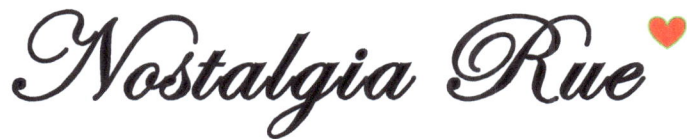

Presents

The Crafty Artisan's™
ARTS & CRAFTS BOOK-A-ZINE

A Guide To DIY Creativity, Personal Development and R.O.I.
A Philosophy of The Indie Arts & Crafts Marketplace

By Mitzi E. Monroe

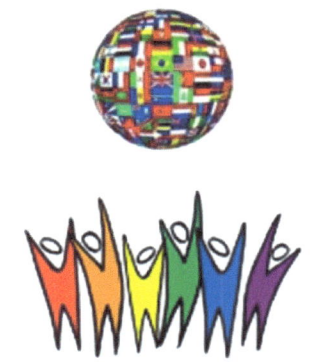

www.nostalgiarue.com

Copyright © 2018 by Mitzi E. Monroe. All Rights Reserved.

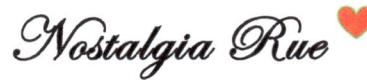

Presents

The Crafty Artisan's™
ARTS & CRAFTS BOOK-A-ZINE

Guide To DIY Creativity, Personal Development and R.O.I.
A Philosophy of The Indie Arts & Crafts Marketplace

9850 S. Maryland Parkway
Suite A-5, P.O. Box # 229
Las Vegas, Nevada 89183
Email: info@nostalgiarue.com
Website: www.nostalgiarue.com

ISBN: 9781726883481

Photo Credits:

Flickr, Wikimedia Commons and The Metropolitan Museum of Art
Adolphe Pierre-Louis, Professional Photographer
Mitzi E. Monroe, Nostalgia Rue

Disclaimer:

The Crafty Artisan™ brand is a division of Nostalgia Rue, a privately owned for-profit multimedia publishing and entertainment company based in Las Vegas, Nevada. Sole proprietor, Mitzi E. Monroe, does not operate a non-profit, 501 (c) (3) organization. For more information, please explore my site and enjoy the possibilities!

~ Mitzi E. Monroe, Founder

All rights reserved. No part of this publication may be reproduced, transmitted, stored in a retrieval system, or used in any form or by any means, graphics, electronic, mechanical, photocopying, recording or otherwise without the prior written permission of the publisher.

Cover (Top Left to Right): Giorgio Vasari (1511-1574): Italian Renaissance Artist/Author, Narcissa Bilack Thorne (1882-1966): American Artist/Miniaturist, Josephine Baker (1906-1975): American born French Entertainer.

Cover (Bottom Left to Right): Henry Ossawa Tanner (1859-1937): An American born French painter, Native American petroglyphs, William Haines (1900-1974): American actor and interior designer.

www.nostalgiarue.com
Copyright © 2018 by Mitzi E. Monroe

DEDICATION/AUTHORS ACKNOWLEDGEMENTS

Thank You Creative Artisans and Crafters!

I would like to acknowledge, thank and dedicate Nostalgia Rue's Crafty Artisan™ Arts & Crafts Book-A-Zine to the hobbyist, indie craft-preneurs and designers who have made the creative DIY movement a wonderful form of self-expression for individuals, an outlet for groups to strengthen community ties and the communities that invest in the shared benefits of an arts and crafts culture that strengthens our humanity and ignited a twenty-first century visual arts renaissance in our lifetime.

Here are a few of my favorite quotes to remind us that the creative journey is an exploration of determination and imagination:

Salvador Dali (1904-1989): A Spanish Surrealist Artist.

"Have no fear of perfection, you'll never reach it."

Barbara Chase-Riboud (1936-   ): An American Sculptor, Novelists and Poet.

"I think our civilization is minimal enough without underlining it. Sculpture as a created object in space should enrich, not reflect, and should be beautiful. Beauty is its function."

Ralph Waldo Emerson (1803-1882): An American Poet and Essayist.

"Every Artist Was First An Amateur."

Henri Matisse (1869-1954): A French Artist.

"Creativity takes courage."

Georgia O'Keefe (1887-1986): An American Artist.

"To create one's own world, in any of the arts, takes courage."

Twyla Tharp (1941-): An American Dancer, Choreographer and Author.

"Art is the only way to run away without leaving home."

The Crafty Artisan's™
ARTS & CRAFTS BOOK-A-ZINE

www.nostalgiarue.com
Copyright © 2018 by Mitzi E. Monroe

Notice

Nostalgia Rue's Crafty Artisan™ Book-A-Zine is intended as a point of reference and inspiration only, not as a known condition of your skill, commitment, or resources to reach your personal artistic abilities. It is sold with the understanding that the author and/or publisher is not engaged in rendering legal, accounting, or other professional services. The information shared here is designed to help you make informed creative decisions based on your approach to your personal goals.

Nothing in this book is intended as an express or implied warranty of the suitability or fitness of any product, service, or program. The reader wishing to use a product, service, or program mentioned in this book does so at their own discretion.

The internet listings and telephone numbers in this book were accurate at the time it went to press. The author or publisher assumes no responsibility for any internet information, addresses or telephone number changes.

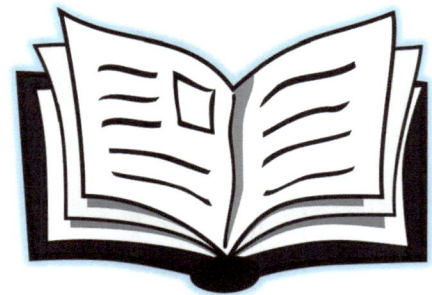

www.nostalgiarue.com

Copyright © 2018 by Mitzi E. Monroe

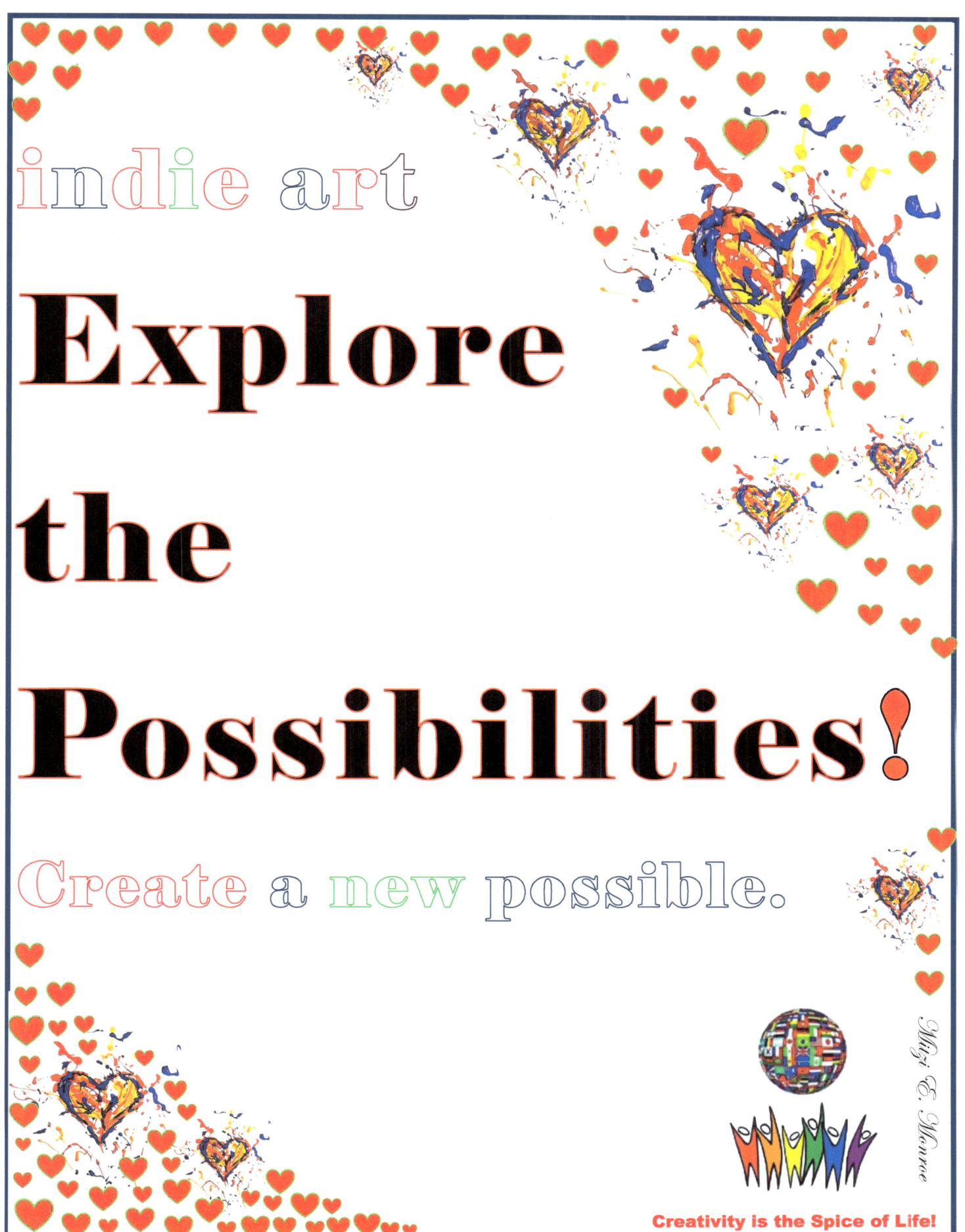

Founder's Message: Inclusivity

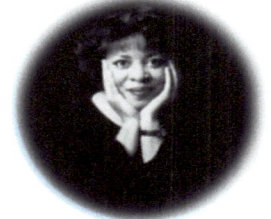
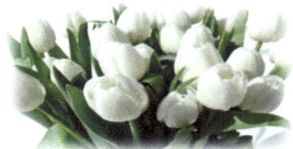
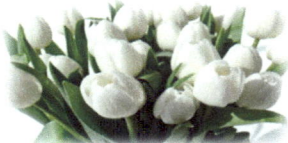
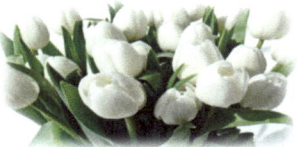

Mitzi E. Monroe, The Crafty Artisan

Thank you for purchasing *Nostalgia Rue Presents The Crafty Artisan's™ Arts & Crafts Book-A-Zine for indie artisans.*

I'm Mitzi E. Monroe, The Crafty Artisan™, an indie craft-preneur, independent living activities specialists, author and visual arts & culture advocate specializing in abstract paper weaving and mixed media paper arts and crafts.

I wrote this book because I couldn't find a local or national organization, books or community-based retailer-artisan initiatives that addresses the reasons why indie craft-preneurs, like myself, have not received inclusion, professional acknowledgment and opportunities for a fair and stable R.O.I. (return on investment) for our artistry and purchasing power as a valued contributing sector of the forty-four billion-dollar DIY arts and crafts industry.

That ignored truth led me on a mission to identify what incentives could motivate the arts and crafts retail chains to collaborate with their entrepreneurial customers, professional and aspiring handmade artisans, to use their common interests to work out shared challenges and align their creative footprints to minimize risk and maximize the seller-customer experience?

Respectfully, it is my personal and professional opinion, no matter how many digital DIY tutorials are uploaded online or how many corporate partnerships are formed in the boardroom, redundant sales and marketing strategies without brick and mortar consumer engagement will not make it possible for local customers, aspiring and talented artisans, to magically turn aspiration hope-filled purchases into a craft-preneurship.

Meaning, indie artisans are set-up to fail, if they lack access to local creative spaces to participate in community collaborations and supportive outlets to plug their creativity into for a sustainable R.O.I.

In no way am I discrediting the efforts of the national organizers of craft fairs, art guilds and First Friday art events who serve a sector of their creative population around the country.

My purpose is to identify what the arts and craft scene lacks for the indie artisans who do not have the same opportunities to develop their skills and/or showcase their diverse talents within their local communities.

Without a focused engagement to reciprocate a holistic approach to the arts and crafts scene, everyone, including retailers, indie and mainstream artisans and their untapped consumer base who are seeking both trendy and unique purchases, we will all collectively eat the failure of an underdeveloped local handmade arts and crafts industry and marketplace.

Yet, the local government business offices, chambers, retailers and commercial online sites who make millions collecting required licensing, membership and service fees have made no concerted effort to adopt innovative changes to their business models to promote and support the indie visual arts and crafts artisans.

Each year there are talented craft-preneurs who will never reach the pinnacles of entrepreneurship beyond a piece of paper that reads *"business license"* or enter a fair playing field that generates a full-time or supplementary income, partially at the fault of an indifferent corporate business culture that eats the whole start-up pie.

Failure and success should be earned equitably.

www.nostalgiarue.com.
Copyright © 2018 by Mitzi E. Monroe

Founder's Message: Inclusivity

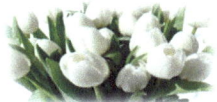 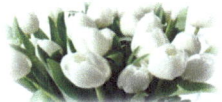 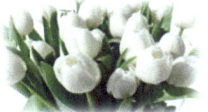

Mitzi E. Monroe, The Crafty Artisan

Without new and old marketplace channels being advocated and collaborated for, jointly, by the arts and craft retail chains, the community, and indie artisans in their shared best interests, craft-preneurs are doomed to experience entry into the market, as a liability rather than an asset, when artisans purchase DIY retail supplies to make their creations in local communities that lack a *handmade to sell* business culture. We can all agree that doesn't make good local investment cents.

So, what does makes sense? It will take fresh ideas that advocate community engagement. Any DIY retailers who want to remain relevant competitors in the arts and crafts marketplace will have to rethink their business model to include local community collaborations with their loyal creative customers.

On the other hand, it's just as important that independent makers of handmade crafts adopt a hybrid indie-commercial business model to promote their indie arts and crafts community, advocate for representation in the business community, and reciprocate their time and knowledge to build creative partnerships with local suppliers and their peers to foster beneficial relationships that strengthens the ethos of the handmade marketplace.

With an understanding of what is required action, I had a lot of questions that needed to move beyond the status quo discussions. The indie community needs a short and long-term action plan? What initiatives can be enacted by the DIY marketplace suppliers and creatives who are ready to cooperate and collaborate in their communities?

In search for the answers, I researched the historical timelines of the artisan beginning with the European renaissance to the development of the American art and craft marketplace, starting with the nineteenth century arts and craft movement to the present day twenty-first century retail DIY arts and craft renaissance, in the United States. I also read a plethora of articles, old and new, that identify the marketplace challenges for retailers, hobbyist and handmade artisans; and I analyzed aspiration hope filled books that romanticize creative entrepreneurship with nowhere for most indie craft artisans to permanently plug their creativity into their local marketplace for direct access to business alignment opportunities, professional development and prospective customers.

www.nostalgiarue.com.
Copyright © 2018 by Mitzi E. Monroe

Founder's Message: Inclusivity

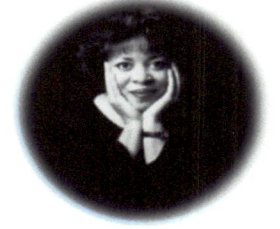

Mitzi E. Monroe, The Crafty Artisan

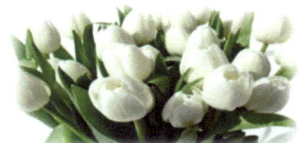 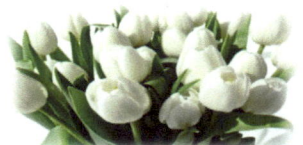 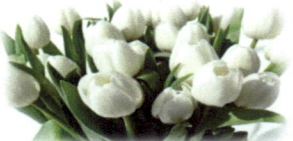

To complete my research, I studied the business and service culture of the arts and craft retail chains, member-based organizations and indie/mainstream craft events, finding that each struggled to find balance between their financial bottom-line and the unique risk factors associated with being an *indie craft-preneur* that happens to be an arts and crafts *customer and/or an organization member.*

Since the arts and crafts industry does not have extensive years of documented data, statistics or media attention specific to the indie visual arts and crafts entrepreneurial history, there is no defense to argue or justify the obvious neglect to acknowledge the DIY hobbyists to handmade artisans creative and financial contributions to the mainstream arts and crafts marketplace have been disregarded.

Moving forward, this book will share the burden equally with the arts and crafts retail chains, city/state business cultures and the hobbyist to artisan entrepreneurs to build a viable mainstream local art and craft culture with an equitable space in the local marketplace for indie artisans in our communities nationwide.

How can this book be of service to help willing participants build a stronger indie arts and craft marketplace culture where all artisans, indie or mainstream makers, can buy supplies to create and sell unique handmade products in their home state?

In a few short words: <u>Act global but think local.</u>

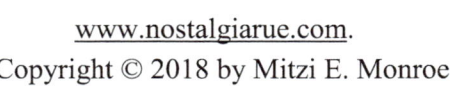

Mitzi E. Monroe,
Craft-preneur

www.nostalgiarue.com.
Copyright © 2018 by Mitzi E. Monroe

The Crafty Artisan's™ ARTS & CRAFTS BOOK-A-ZINE

About This Book-a-zine

Before we move to the mini-zine section, I would first like to clarify what this book-a-zine is and is not about:

1). The Crafty Artisan™ Arts & Crafts Book-a-zine is a hybrid book and magazine with three essential sections:

   - **Section I**: Features
   - **Section II:** Multi-Cultural Arts & Entertainment Mini-Zine
   - **Section III:** The Crafty Artisans™ Arts & Crafts Inspiration Directory

2). This book does not promote aspirational promises of hope that hard work, talent and a craft store checklist, alone, will guarantee small handmade business success in today's forty-four billion-dollar arts & craft marketplace.

3). This book speaks to the arts and craft industry openly and honestly by proposing one of my solution driven ideas to nurture and benefit all vested parties collectively based on today's DIY culture.

4). This book is for artisans who want to understand how to avoid diving in head first, keep overhead costs at a minimum and steer clear of romanticizing what being an indie craft-preneur is not.

5). This books purpose is not to repeat easy steps to entrepreneurship fail for the average hobbyist to artisan but offer insight on what common barriers exist and how to build a support system for those who wish to generate a revenue stream by building an arts and craft community based on a common goal to collaborate and see the bigger picture for a reciprocal creative purpose.

It's very rare a generation has an opportunity to raise the standards required to change what time requires of its subjects inter-collectively.

Nostalgia Rue's Crafty Artisan's'™ *Guide to DIY Creativity, Personal Development and R.O.I. A Philosophy of The Indie Arts & Crafts Marketplace* is a bookshelf staple for inspiration, tough support and creative suggestions I'm happy to share with you about building an indie arts and craft community offline.

www.nostalgiarue.com
Copyright © 2018 by Mitzi E. Monroe

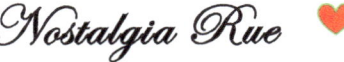

The Crafty Artisan's™
ARTS & CRAFTS BOOK-A-ZINE

A Guide To DIY Creativity, Personal Development and R.O.I.
A Philosophy of The Indie Arts & Crafts Marketplace

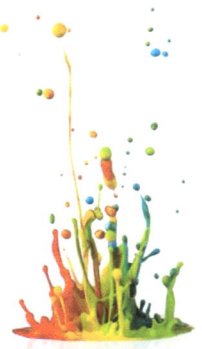

Contents

Introduction: Founders Message 6
About This Book-A-Zine 9

Features 11

Art 101: The Great American Arts & Crafts Story: People, Places & Cultural Ideas 11
Game Changers: Engage As You Age 19
The Harlem Renaissance: An Influential Movement in American Art History 20
Final Thoughts & Suggestions 22

Multi-Cultural Art & Entertainment Blog-A-Zine 23

From the Heart: A Letter From the Founder 25
Creative Spotlight: Edith Head (cover) 26
Mitzi's 50+ Hers & His Beauty & Grooming Picks 27
Destination Las Vegas: Arts & Culture Calendar 29
Entertainment Market Report 30
Nostalgic Recipe Vault: Slumgullion Stew 31
Favorite Classic Art & Culture 32
Creative Literature & Film 33
Dear Betty White: Nostalgia Rue's 2018 American Arts & Crafts "Icon" Award Recipient 34
Classic Network Television Station Guide 36

The Crafty Artisan's™ Arts & Crafts Inspiration Directory 37

Books 39
Film 39
Internet 40
Media: TV/Radio/Podcast 40
Multicultural Art & Film Enthusiasts Multimedia Culture Series 41
Thank You! 42

www.nostalgiarue.com
Copyright © 2018 by Mitzi E. Monroe

Section I: The Great American Arts & Craft Story: People, Places and Cultural Ideas.

How do you identify with your creative persona? Are you an artist, artisan, a crafter or visual artist, in the arts and crafts or the visual arts field?

I get asked the same questions and for argument's sake, my professional title, the Crafty Artisan™, speaks to my creativity, my innovative spirit and my works as a visual arts and craft artisan.

To answer the question more directly, I personally believe it takes artistry and craftsmanship to create handmade works of art for aesthetic and/or functional purpose. Both.

I feel artistry is the personal visual style and imagination of the artisan and the craftsmanship is the mastered technique and overall workmanship.

So where did the word artist, artisan and crafter come from? In my pursuit for an answer, it puzzled me why Etsy-preneurs with handmade DIY Vlogs, on YouTube, per my knowledge, are not tackling the *"art or craft,"* professional vs. non-professional debate comparisons from long ago.

It's a valid question and concern that warrants an answer when so many indie makers are flooding the online platforms in overcrowded categories with copycat creations that offer few opportunities to promote and sell their handmade creations for pleasure or stable cash flow, when many are competing for online eyeballs for economic survival offline.

With an uncontainable curiosity, I decided to explore the root and conditions that feeds this multi-sided debate. My motivation is not to change anyone's word preferences, but to provide an understanding and appreciation for individual creativity whether it's categorized as mainstream or an indie handmade work of art.

After all, the Great American Arts & Crafts Story has always been shrouded in the passionate debate for who should be deemed an artist, an artisan or a crafter in creative circles in the United States.

I found reasons that go back to the first renaissance period in Italy, that spread throughout Europe and the United States to search for the roots of the ongoing artist-crafter debate.

That debate is also heavily influenced by the arts and crafts suppliers who set the pace for the latest trends per the variety of mediums available, colors and the latest products, techniques and equipment available online and at your local big box specialty stores like Joann's, Hobby Lobby and Michael's.

The Crafty Artisan's™ ARTS & CRAFTS BOOK-A-ZINE

Section I: The Great American Arts & Crafts Story: People, Places, Cultures and Ideas.

Here are the most common reasons why the debate continues today, present to past:

6). <u>History</u>: When we think of art most of us envision museum exhibits of famous paintings like the Mona Lisa portrait by Italian renaissance painter Leonardo da Vinci (1452-1519), the Cellini Salt Cellar sculpture by Benvenuto Cellini (1500-1571) or archeological finds from historical landmarks around the world predating America.

5). <u>Retail</u>: The big box retail chains dictate frequent trends that define arts & craft pop culture for mass-produced DIY products that lack grade A quality for lower pricing, a short shelf life and a fiercely competitive handmade marketplace online.

4). Classic or Modern (*21st Century Renaissance*): There are many mediums in the categorization of arts and crafts: Paint, glass, mixed media, clay, wood, metal, stone or textiles which some creatives consider hand made creations for aesthetic and domestic use as modern or contemporary crafts vs. fine art grade supplies and antiquities for investment and classic collection purposes as art.

3). <u>Training</u>: A fine arts degree versus self-taught?

2). <u>The Renaissance</u> (1300-1600s): The renaissance is the rebirth period or revival of art and literature in Europe following the medieval period between the 13th and 16th centuries. Around the 1400s the renaissance humanism period was popularized in Florence, Italy before spreading throughout Europe. Renaissance humanism is a movement that acknowledged individual creativity and worth, hence the *word artist* was created during humanism for painters, sculptors and architects who successfully proposed their patron commissioned works be paid based on merit and their individual artistry instead of the medieval collective payment system that continued for *artisans* who did not receive professional credit or individual pay for their handmade hats, jewelry, Goldsmith or stone masonry workmanship. *Hence, the* artist vs. crafter designations and start of the ongoing debate.

1). <u>Giorgio Vasari</u> (1511-1574): Giorgio Vasari was an Italian painter, architect, writer, and historian, most famous today for penning the first art history book, *"Lives of the Most Excellent Painters, Sculptors, and Architects,"* published in 1550. Over four centuries later, his book remains in print.

www.nostalgiarue.com
Copyright © 2018 by Mitzi E. Monroe

Section I: The Great American Arts & Crafts Story: People, Places, Cultures and Ideas.

The previous short list considers the complexities that evolves around the designation of artist, artisan or crafter which spans from the late 14th-century renaissance period in Europe to the present day, highlighting seven-hundred and eighteen years of man's humanity in art history communicated through various creative mediums, debates and values for each role in the United States arts and craft culture.

The great American arts and craft story cannot be told without acknowledging its European roots where master painters, sculptors and architects, like Fresco painter Fra Angelico (1395-1455), became artists noted for their individual works during the renaissance period that began in Florence, Italy, long before Christopher Columbus (1451-1506) explored the Americas in 1492, and the first European settlers landed in Jamestown, Virginia (May 1607) and the Plymouth Colony (1620-1691).

Just as the renaissance (rebirth) humanist period brought light, humanity and individual merit and pay for Italian artists for their individual works, a departure from the previous period of medieval workshops, much of that credit is due to a painter who would not reach the pinnacle success of his friend, painter, Michelangelo, but who would find his own literary and architectural legacy by immortalizing two-hundred Italian "artists" with the first art history book about renaissance painters, sculptors and architects personal and professional biographies that spanned the thirteenth, fourteenth and fifteenth centuries.

That person is Giorgio Vasari (1511-1574), a 16th- century painter, architect and historical writer recognized as the first art historian and inventor of the encyclopedia of artistic biographies for his book, *Lives of the Most Excellent Painters, Sculptors, and Architects*," published in 1550 and reprinted during his lifetime in 1568. This remarkable publication is the renaissance humanist periods literary record of the first official artists', the rebirth of art creativity, culture and individual worth that set the standards for a collective modern culture movement that would define *fine art*.

I was also fascinated by and impressed with the medieval and renaissance period master artists' tradition to help apprentices and journeymen move up the ranks with years of practice and experience to ensure they too reached master status in their trade to pass down their handmade craftsmanship for future generations.

The seventeenth century European settlers who braved the harsh Atlantic Ocean voyage would have to use their creative wits and imagination to conquer the undeveloped North American land in the new world they would struggle to rebuild future lives.

Section I: The Great American Arts & Crafts Story: People, Places, Cultures and Ideas.

If you're wondering about the 17th century artists and artisans arriving from Europe to the first colonies, most were too busy with sickness and death before the surviving colonists, between 1616-1699, learned their fortunes lay in growing and trading tobacco, cotton and furs with England for furniture, tools, clothing, food and other goods from the London Company (*aka Virginia Company of London; est. 1607*) than finding gold, silver and copper in the Virginia hills of the Americas.

Before European colonization in the new world, art existed with the indigenous tribal traditions of Native American art and Spanish colonization's (1492-1898) architectural influences, mainly in North America's south and southwest territories.

Eventually as settlers became acquainted with the land and built new communities between the late 17th and early 18th centuries colonial period, America's early art consisted of a painting or paper portraiture by visiting European artists commissioned by wealthy families, a few explorer drawn maps and depicted images of Native American tribes, popular handicrafts *(furniture, pottery, glassware, etc.)*, lithographs and the only seventeenth-century New England painting that is clearly linked to a known painter and mariner, Captain Thomas Smith's self-portrait (c. 1689), is the only surviving canvas of that period with linkage to an American self-portrait.

There are three American artists who became leading visionaries for their expressions of American Colonial art and its historical relevance during the 18th and 19th century. The First and the most famous and influential American born colonial artist is Benjamin West (1738-1820) for his 1770 oil painting, depicting *The Death of British General James Wolfe* (1727-1759) in modern dress during the Seven Year's War between Britain and France, a war that would determine the fate of Frances North American colonies. West became America's first and most famous painter to garner international fame and establish a historical genre in American art for his masterpiece.

The next artist was a student of Benjamin West, Charles Wilson Peale (1741-1827), is best remembered for portrait paintings of American Revolutionaries and historic figures, including his most famous being the first portraiture artist to paint George Washington several times, Benjamin Franklin, John Hancock, Thomas Jefferson and Alexander Hamilton.

The Crafty Artisan's™ ARTS & CRAFTS BOOK-A-ZINE

Section I: The Great American Arts & Crafts Story: People, Places, Cultures and Ideas.

Mr. Peale is also founder of the Pennsylvania Academy of the Fine Arts Museum and School (1805), know today as the known as Peale's American Museum, known as the oldest art museum and art school in the United States.

Just as importantly, we must remember Gilbert Charles Stuart (1755-1828) an American portraitist from Rhode Island to be considered one of America's best portraitist, painter of the first six U.S. Presidents and a savvy entrepreneur in his day. Mr. Stuart retained an unfinished portrait of George Washington and used it to paint 130 copies that he sold for $100.00 each. That image of President George Washington (1796) is featured on the United States one-dollar bill and the 19th and early 20th century U.S. postage stamps. He also painted John Trumbull (1756-1843), in 1818, famous for the *Declaration of Independence* painting purchased by the United States Congress, along with his *Surrender of General Burgoyne.*

During this period, American architects of the colonial era were influenced by the popular King George *Georgian designs* of England's Thomas Chippendale (1718-1779) furniture or the Neoclassical architectural designs favored by early American architects, including our third President, Thomas Jefferson (1743-1829) and Charles-Louis Clérisseau (1721-1820), who designed the Virginia State Capitol, with the building's completion in 1785. Overall, the Neoclassical and Georgian influences defined the United States aesthetics of a newly formed United States to present day both residential and commercial buildings.

Between the late 19th century and early 20th century, art had taken on a pivotal role in shaping and chronicling American work and leisure history. Creating many opportunities for artists, crafters and designers to pursue entrepreneurial ventures in: vaudeville stage performances, printing for self-promotion, portrait photography studios were commonplace, art galleries and museums were opening, art schools for instruction were established and handmade crafts were available via mail order. It was a time for innovation in the United States of America.

www.nostalgiarue.com
Copyright © 2018 by Mitzi E. Monroe

Section I: The Great American Arts & Crafts Story: People, Places, Cultures and Ideas.

The Industrial Revolution (1760-1840s) was the most important period in living history as we know it today. Without the industrial revolution, which began in Britain, the United States would not have successfully transitioned from limited hand production methods into a modern standard of living without the machines and tools that developed the factory system that fueled mass production for the twenty-first century products, transportation and convenient services that 326.5 million "Americans" take for granted in our daily lives in the U.S.A.

Looking back, the Industrial Revolution ignited an international decorative and fine arts movement in Britain called the Arts and Craft Movement, between 1880 and 1920, that spread throughout Europe, America and Japan. Traditional hand craftsmen saw their livelihoods challenged or abolished and complained massed produced crafts did not create a superior quality of work or standards in mechanized productions which became a catalyst for economic and social reform that advocated for new enforced labor laws.

For surviving handmade artisans of the industrial revolution like Britain's, William Morris (1834-1896), the most prolific figure and influencer in the 19th century Arts and Craft anti-industrial movement, developed a personal style to make award-winning handmade furniture and interiors in the British countryside design using medieval period techniques.

The American version of the Arts and Crafts movement less resembled the rustic British anti-industrialization movement for a simpler more refined decorative aesthetic to design middle-class targeted homes in the new consumer focused industrialized manufacturing culture. A compromise to blend the best of both worlds furnishings and decorative pieces made using machinery, tools and handmade craftsmanship.

On January 05, 1897, the first American Arts and Craft Society met and organized their first exhibition in Boston on April 05, 1897. More than 1000 objects were made by craftsmen with half of the makers being women.

I believe this effort has a lot to do with a slow but coming of age concept for artists guilds, creative art classes and fairs for today's modern DIY arts and craft industry.

www.nostalgiarue.com
Copyright © 2018 by Mitzi E. Monroe

Section I: The Great American Arts & Crafts Story: People, Places, Cultures and Ideas.

It would behoove me not to mention America's own Arts and Craft Movement influencer, Gustav Stickley (1858-1942). Gustav Stickley was the most important American furniture designer, manufacturer and publisher of The American Craftsman magazine (1900-1901) and American Craftsman styles extension of William Morris' simplistic style during the arts and craft movement in Britain. Stickley encouraged his customers to create their own handmade aesthetics for the home in his magazine. He was an advocate of the DIY arts and craft movement. Today Stickley's 1901 and 1904 pieces are rare collectibles.

The Museum of the American Arts and Crafts Movement is slated to open in 2019 in St. Petersburg, Florida.

So how did European fine arts and the arts and craft movement evolve into a twenty-first century handmade arts and craft marketplace in the United States?

Actually, there have always been individuals or groups making things by hand to make their daily lives simpler or to sell or trade since the first settlers arrived in Jamestown. There's always been handmade crafts that have been passed down from generation to generation: quilting, painting, making candles, homemade candy, sewing, jewelry and toy makers. The possibilities are endless!

What's different is we are experiencing a twenty-first century arts and craft renaissance that has expanded from DIY furniture to home décor that includes artisan foods and libations. Life is art!

People are searching television how-to-shows, reading artisan publications and watching their favorite DIY channel on YouTube for inspiration.

Based on a persons interests and skill set, almost anything can be made if you have the investment, passion and space. But it wouldn't be possible if not for the specialty arts and craft stores like Joann's (1943-), Hobby Lobby (1970-) and Michael's Arts & Crafts (1976-); the top three largest arts and craft DIY supply chains in America.

The Crafty Artisan's™ ARTS & CRAFTS BOOK-A-ZINE

Section I: The Great American Arts & Crafts Story: People, Places, Cultures and Ideas.

We have to give credit to the DIY instructors who keep their creative spirits on the pulse of the latest how-to-trends or share their own signature creations with hobbyist and aspiring craft-preneurs in-person at community meeting spaces, if you're lucky to have one at your disposal or online.

What enthusiast are learning can be recreated to spruce up their homes, as customized gifts or to launch a small handmade business online, at craft shows and wholesale opportunities. Thanks to the convenience of global suppliers and shared information, the arts and craft industry has exploded.

What I've noticed in my research and from my own experience as a handmade artisan that is missing are local arts and craft chains are not engaging their indie craft-preneurs beyond a transactional relationship. With a corporate bottom-line business model to sell, sell and sell more, aspiring craft-preneurs need a modern day arts and craft movement that nurtures indie artisans.

Remember two things, people can't buy your crafts if they haven't heard of it and starting a handmade business isn't a business if you have no where to plug your creativity into for a R.O.I. (return on investment).

JOANN's concept store in Columbus, Ohio has answered the call by offering its local artisan space to self-promote with a handmade market in-store, equipment rentals and space to learn new crafts and make their own in the store. It's being tested for now, but I'm excited to see such a concept spread nationwide. Article by Megan Green, July 02, 2018 (Article: Joann Opens Concept Store in Columbus, Ohio)

I hope learning about art history from the perspective of an indie arts and craft-preneur will inspire you to connect with one another to create spaces where your generation of artisans can help each other build an indie handmade culture in your local communities. Every arts and crafts movement not only requires creativity, as evidenced by movements in the past, but a committed effort by local retailers, indie artisans and community spaces collectively. The pride and economic benefits is the true bottom-line.

www.nostalgiarue.com
Copyright © 2018 by Mitzi E. Monroe

Game Changers

Engage As You Age, LLC

Ben Lewis, MA, Engage As You Age, Founder

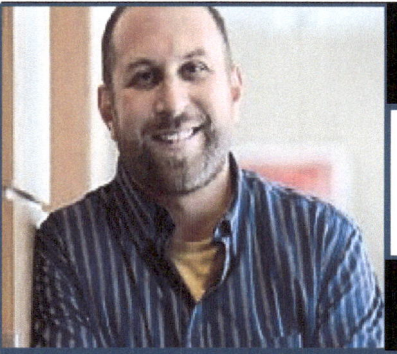

If I placed "Game Changer" in the middle of this page and just listed Ben Lewis' photo and company name, "Engage As you Age," he'd have nothing more to prove. Mr. Lewis has put his finger on the pulse of a social need just as important as medical care: Engagement through human contact.

Ben is the founder of, Engage As You Age, a home visit service that engages home-alone older persons wanting and needing social interactions for companionship to enhance their routine medical plans of care and healing benefits.

Ben's 2008 start-up is an American dream with a princely fairytale come true. In 2005, Ben replied to a Craigslist ad to visit with an elderly woman, Anna Garlund, in a Japantown retirement community for companionship. The two shared an interest in history. Lewis earned an M.A. in African studies at Yale. With each visit their bond grew stronger and developed into a friendship.

In Garlund's obituary, her family requested contributions be sent to Lewis so that he could start a service working with seniors. A loving gift turned into the first service of its kind, Engage As You Age, based in San Francisco, California. Engage As You Age hires the best "Activity Specialists" that are trained and matched with seniors of vast experiences and interests from the arts to nuclear energy. And sometimes they just want to visit to talk about whatever is on their minds.

Ten years later, Engage As You Age has brought many home alone seniors reciprocated friendship and improved quality of life through good listening, sharing mutual interests, and checking off learning new things in on bucket list.

Today, Ben admits he's learned a lot about the long term care industry and the services available to older persons. He's become the "go to" person for aging in his community. And he's proven there is always a way to stay connected in later life.

Contact Engage As You Age if you live in the greater San Francisco area and would like to learn more about their one-on-one services and group activities.

Engage As You Age, LLC
275 5th Street, Suite 201
San Francisco, CA 94103
Phone: 415-690-6944
Fax: 415-541-8588
Website: www.engageasyouage.com

THE HARLEM RENAISSANCE:
An Influential Movement in American Art History

When we think of the Harlem Renaissance, most of us can remember our formal years in school reciting a Langston Hughes poem, that familiar poem that would become the inspiration for writer and playwright Lorraine Hansberry's play, *A Raisin in the Sun*, titled:

Harlem

(What Happens To A Dream Deferred?)

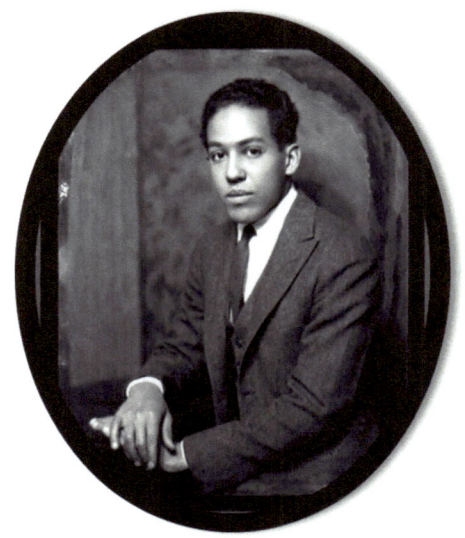

By Harlem Renaissance Poet, Langston Hughes (1902-1967)

What happens to a dream deferred?

**Does it dry up
Like a raisin in the sun?**

**Or fester like a sore--
And then run?**

**Does it stink like rotten meat?
Or crust and sugar over--
like a syrupy sweet?**

**Maybe it just sags
like a heavy load.**

Or does it explode?

www.nostalgiarue.com
Copyright © 2018 by Mitzi E. Monroe

THE HARLEM RENAISSANCE:
An Influential Movement in American Art History

Langston Hughes "Harlem," depicts the cultural movement expressed through artistic, intellectual and social storytellers who used many creative mediums to record the American dreams and hopes that were compromised or deferred for twentieth century Native Black American D.O.S. *(descendant of slaves)*, during the great migration, from the rural southern United States, between 1916 and the 1930s, to find work and a better life for their families in urban cities in northern and Midwestern states with majority black enclaves in Harlem, New York, Philadelphia, Boston and Chicago allowed them to distance themselves from racial degradation and segregation laws known as Jim Crow in the southern United States.

The city of Harlem, an upper Manhattan borough in New York, had the largest concentration of the six-million southern Native Black American migrants living in the area during this period. As a result, the cultural movement that ensued would be called the Harlem Renaissance or the "New Negro Movement."

The Harlem Renaissance represented a new birth for children and grandchildren of slaves. A blossoming mecca with opportunities for educated Native Black American professional's to serve their communities as doctors and teachers. And many more opened mom-and-pop store front businesses for Harlem's majority black population. Harlem quickly became a bustling community reminiscent of the Black Wall Street (1906-1921) in Greenwood, Oklahoma outside of Tulsa before the government bombed the city and nearby white citizens burned it down in the 1921 summer massacre.

Although the new northerners fresh start did not mirror the same equal parts freedom or wealth as their white counterparts, it was less oppressive in comparison to the southern states they had fled. Most found jobs as domestics, laborers in industrial plants or any job that supported a life in Harlem.

Some former residents of *Black Wall Street* fled to Harlem, famous for its visual artists community where works of art told their stories, home of the landmark whites only night club, The Cotton Club, made it possible for rich white patrons to meet and finance black artisans whose works expressed the black DOS experience and their humanity.

For the artist, creating their works were often a financial challenge to bring into fruition with menial jobs between new pieces and limited output. For the Harlem Renaissance artisans like poet Langston Hughes, author and anthropologist Zora Neale Hurston and painter Aaron Douglas with wealthy white patron, Charlotte Osgood Mason *(aka God Mother)*, friendship with photographer Carl Van Vechten and philanthropists William E. Hurston and Julius Rosenwald, sometimes meant limited control over what they produced and servitude.

Never-the-less, what is evident is, the Harlem Renaissances culture movement beautifully celebrates the Native Black American D.O.S. courage and accomplishments that is treasured in national archives, books and films to never forget the artistry of life achieved in the tapestry of Native Black America's greatest migration in history.

www.nostalgiarue.com
Copyright © 2018 by Mitzi E. Monroe

My Final Thoughts & Suggestions:

As promised, I'm concluding the book portion of this book-a-zine with my final thoughts and a suggestion you can use, as promised, in my introduction. I feel it's just as important to address the issues but share helpful marketing and self-promotion tips in every edition. We all know potential customers can't find you if they haven't heard of you.

My suggestion matches my passion for the arts and culture. A passion that developed into an advocacy to build new paths to craft-preneurship for small indie artisans through solution driven collaborations offline.

My solution summarizes everything I wrote in this book in two words: Community and collaboration. I hinted at community several times in this hybrid book and magazine concoction, of what and why, to suggest how we can DIY our way out of the obscure indie handmade shadows and into the light of discovery, development and R.O.I.

My suggestions encourage local retailers and craft event organizers, indie artists, crafters and designers to form local community collaborations. A commitment to collaborate at least one annual event or activity that caters to what the market can bare. That doesn't mean having the biggest and the costliest affair, bombarding events with copycat knockoffs or ruthless competition. My ideas are focused on collective marketing and self-promotion events with shared costs at the lowest minimum risk.

Come together, as a community, to enhance an existing event or create a new one that is inclusive to all local creatives. Here are my suggestions for enhancing or creating new arts & crafts events:

Craft Fairs: Offer a small professional mini workshop for artisans during the first 90 minutes of the fair.

Festivals: Create with a purpose. Have attendees donate $5 to assemble DIY Arts & Crafts Kits for kids in shelters, hospitals and/or daycares.

Retail Stores: Invite local indie artisans to participate in a holiday in-store swag bag give-a-way event with a $1 submission fee to help donate arts and crafts supplies for a local youth program or community outreach effort.

Indie Artisans: To avoid over extending yourselves financially to keep up with several shows a year, advocate for community inspired marketing events to self-promote via collective collaborations like the above to reach consumers and direct them to your website. Marketing this way once or twice a year can promote who you are, what you offer and where you'll be on and offline, for example:

- Promote yourself beyond a business card by having a small 8.5 x 5.5 flier with your craft show calendar, website and an image of your top seller.

- Volunteer to reciprocate and build a relationship with your craft-preneur community.

- Plan ahead and purchase supplies to create your inventory off season for great discounts.

- Share a booth until you're able to build a customer base, figure out your bestsellers and can make sells on your website.

Nostalgia Rue

MULTI-CULTURAL ARTS & ENTERTAINMENT

Fall/Winter Blog-a-zine 2018-2019

REMEMBERING
EDITH HEAD
HOLLYWOOD STUDIO
COSTUME FASHION ICON

ART & CULTURE
UNLIMITED CHOICES

SLUMGULLION STEW
NOSTALGIC RECIPE VAULT

THE **HARLEM** RENAISSANCE

DESTINATION LAS VEGAS
ARTS & CULTURAL CALENDAR

PLUS!

A NOSTALGIA RUE EXCLUSIVE

The Crafty Artisan's™
Indie Arts & Craft Inspiration Directory

A Guide to D.I.Y. Creativity
Professional Development
and R.O.I. Resources

50+ HIS & HERS
BEAUTY & GROOMING PICKS

THE ENTERTAINMENT MARKET REPORT

ART 101: ARTIST OR CRAFTER?

Nostalgia Rue's
The Crafty Artisan™
ARTS & CRAFT MINI-ZINE

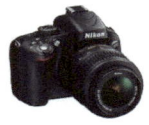 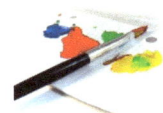 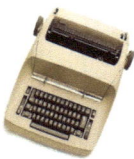 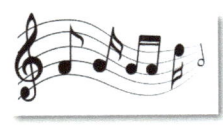

CONTENTS

Multi-Cultural Art & Entertainment Blog-a-Zine 23

From the Heart: A Letter From the Founder 25
Creative Spotlight: Edith Head (cover) 26
Mitzi's 50+ Hers & His Beauty & Grooming Picks 27
Destination Las Vegas: Arts & Culture Calendar 29
Entertainment Market Report 30
Nostalgic Recipe Vault: Slumgullion Stew 31
Favorite Classic Art & Culture 32
Creative Literature & Film 33
Dear Betty White: Nostalgia Rue's 2018 American Arts & Craft "Icon" Award Recipient 34
Classic Network Television Station Guide 36

The Crafty Artisan's™ Arts & Crafts Inspiration Directory 37

Books 39
Film 39
Internet 40
Media: TV/Radio 40
Multicultural Art & Film Enthusiasts Multimedia Culture Series 41
Thank You! 42

FROM THE HEART: A LETTER FROM THE FOUNDER

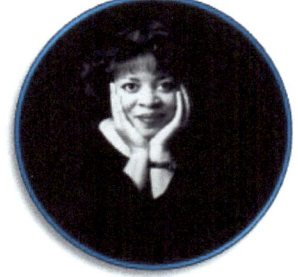 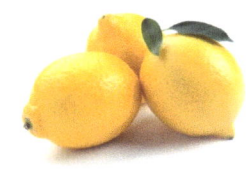 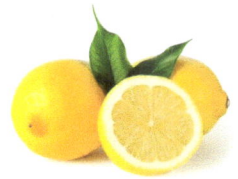 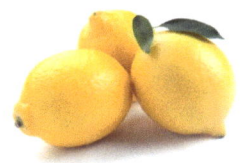

Let Me Entertain You! Multi-Cultural Art, Culture & Entertainment

Welcome to the First Entertainment Edition of Nostalgia Rue's Crafty Artisan™ Book-A-Zine!

I am so happy and blessed to know in the midst of an unsettling economy, horrific weekly news reports and the challenges faced by creative solo-craft-preneurs or sole proprietors like myself, to launch a small arts and craft publication in a big corporate pond, I am proud to introduce Nostalgia Rue's clear vision to serve and support indie artisans who are working diligently to deliver the past to present their creative interpretations of twenty-first century life.

The Crafty Artisan's™ Arts & Crafts Blog-a-zine is Nostalgia Rue's arts and cultural arm of this book-a-zine. Nostalgia Rue, a multimedia publishing and digital entertainment company, has combined my curiosity for art history with present day arts and craft culture to publish a hybrid magazine and book to help both hobbyist and artisan's get inspired by past and present creative themes to find their personal style, connect with persons who are seeking or want to share information, services and social engagement opportunities individually or in group settings for today's art and craft enthusiasts.

Each issue I will share with you what my curiosity introduces me to. The pages of this blog-a-zine will be an exploration of entertainment, art and culture at best. I'm also empowered to advocate that art should be a self-expression of fun, therapeutic escapism and a historical account of the times.

Reaching back to the past, I've always admired Edith Head, the Hollywood costume fashion designer's determination become a movie studio costume designer. Edith Head's road to success is a solid example of reinvention and innovative strategy exemplified. A pioneering example of career vision and staying power. The creative spotlight for the entertainment cover story, featuring Edith Head, tells her story of how her enthusiasm to learn costume design, work hard and share her advancing talents to sustain a fifty-year career, that served both her needs and her fellow industry mates for a legacy that lives on in classic movie history. I hope Edith's story and the pages of her triumphs will inspire you to reach out as you continue to find meaningful ways to spread more sunshine, motivation and can-do spirit to seek creative ways to stay engaged with any and every art medium you explore.

The Spring/Summer 2019 edition will be published in March. When interests demands a more frequent printing, I will publish a special quarterly book-a-zine vs. the Fall/Winter and Spring/Summer editions.

Please feel free to tour my website to learn more about Nostalgia Rue and find out what's new, what's old and what's about to happen!

Enjoy!

Mitzi E. Monroe, Independent Living Activities Specialist & Indie Artisan Advocate

www.nostalgiarue.com
Copyright © 2018 by Mitzi E. Monroe

EDITH HEAD

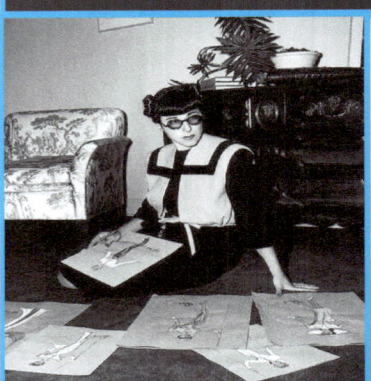 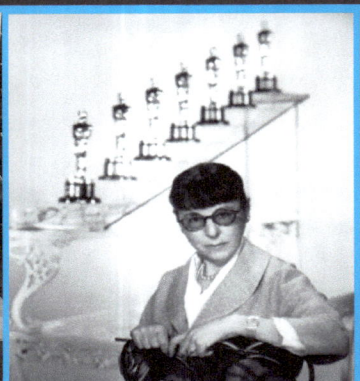 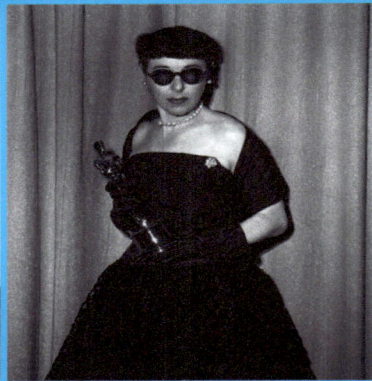 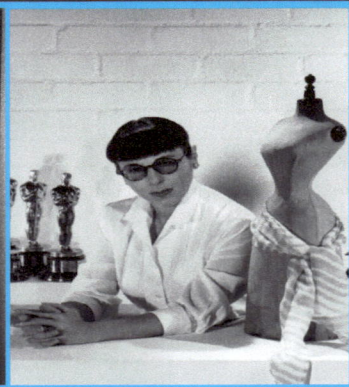

HOLLYWOOD COSTUME FASHION LEGEND

Edith Head (1897-1981) was born in the late 19th century at a time when Hollywood was just inventing itself, first with motion toys to five cent Nicklelodeon theaters in 1905.

In 1911, when Edith was a 14 year old teenager, Nestor Motion Picture Company made the first Hollywood motion picture. Edith's teens and young adult period in southern California must have been abuzz about the new glamorous film industry. By the time Hollywood had established a firm hold on the new film industry, Edith had received her bachelor of arts degree in letters and science with honors in French from the University of California, Berkeley, and in 1920 she earned a master of arts degree in romance languages from Stanford University. She became a French language teacher in La Jolla and took a new position teaching French one year later at the Hollywood School for Girls. Edith knew she wanted to be a sketch artist for Paramount. To earn more money, she told the Hollywood School for Girls she could teach art. Although she had only taken lessons in high school, she went to night school to improve her drawing skills at the Chouinard Art College. She met and married her art classmates brother, Charles Head, in 1923.

In 1924, Edith didn't let a lack of art, design or costume design experience derail her from applying and getting a costume sketch artist position at Paramount Pictures in their costume design department. In a documentary, Edith admits borrowing other art students' best drawings as her portfolio for her job interview. Once hired it was evident she lacked the total package.

By Mitzi E. Monroe. Author and Founder of Nostalgia Rue.

What she did have was moxie. The studio recognized her passion and ambition to mentor her. With hard work and good people skills, Edith established herself as one of Hollywood's go to leading costume designers. She worked for Paramount for 43 years. In 1967, she moved to Universal.

At this time Edith had divorced and married set designer, Wiard Ihnen, in 1940 until his passing in 1979. Edith Head's career spans the history of the golden years of Hollywood into the late 20th century. Her last major film was, "The Sting," with Paul Newman and Robert Redford in 1973. She received her final Oscar for The Sting in 1974.

Edith Head passed away on October 24, 1981 at age 83, from an incurable bone marrow disease, myelofibrosis. She was laid to rest at Forest Lawn Memorial Park in Glendale, California.

Edith Head remains etched in our memories by the plethora of Hollywood history, the countless stars we see fashioned in her designs on TCM movies, books she authored and video tributes streaming online.

There will never be another Edith Head. We're so fortunate we have her fabulosity preserved forever.

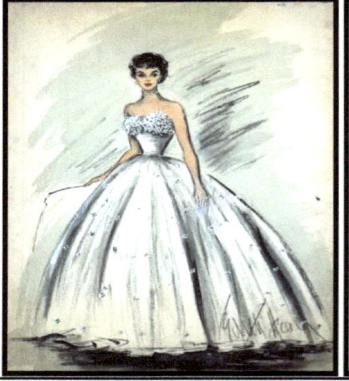 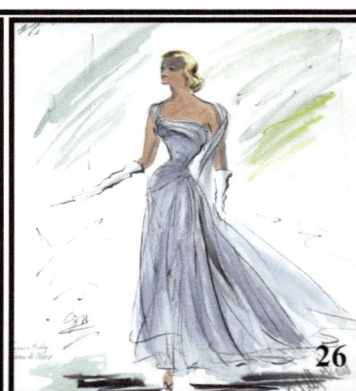

Mitzi's Head to Toe Beauty Picks

"Pour yourself a drink, put on some lipstick, and pull yourself together." ~ Elizabeth Taylor

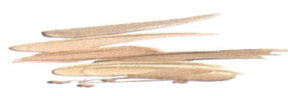 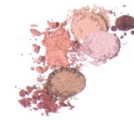 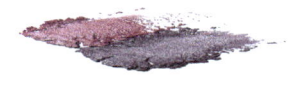 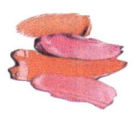

Face: Primer

Avon's MagiX Face Perfector is dematologists tested to be used as a primer over moisturizer and under foundation to blur away natures imperfections before applying makeup. Has an SPF of 20 to protect your skin for days you prefer to go au natural.

Avon: www.avon.com

Hair: Thinning Hair

KERANIQUE'S SCALP STIMULATING SHAMPOO
Fortified with the KERANIQUE Amino Complex for our best Volumizing Shampoo

Contact: https://keranique.com/scalp-stimulating-shampoo-for-thinning-hair

Body: Healing Moisturizer

Keri Shea Butter Conditioning Therapy Lotion

Retailer: Walgreen's

Scents: Romantic Soft Scent for a Signature Fragrance

Lancome Eau de Parfum Spray

Retailer: Nordstrom's

Nails & Feet: D.Y.I. Mani-Pedi Travel Kit

Beauty School Mani-Pedi Kit—SBS-156990

Retailer: Sallybeauty.com

Internet Makeup Tips:

Boom! By Cindy Joseph: www.boombycindyjoseph.com
Boomers life after 50: www.aboomerslifeafter50.com
Over 50 Feeling 40: www.over50feeling40.com

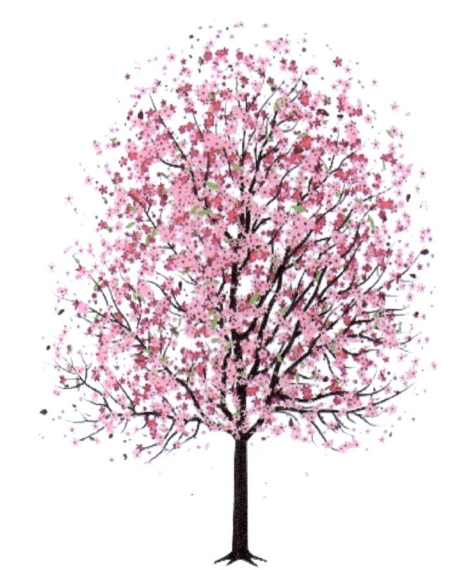

www.nostalgiarue.com Copyright © 2018 by Mitzi E. Monroe.

Nostalgia Rue's Classic Spring-Summer Selections For Men

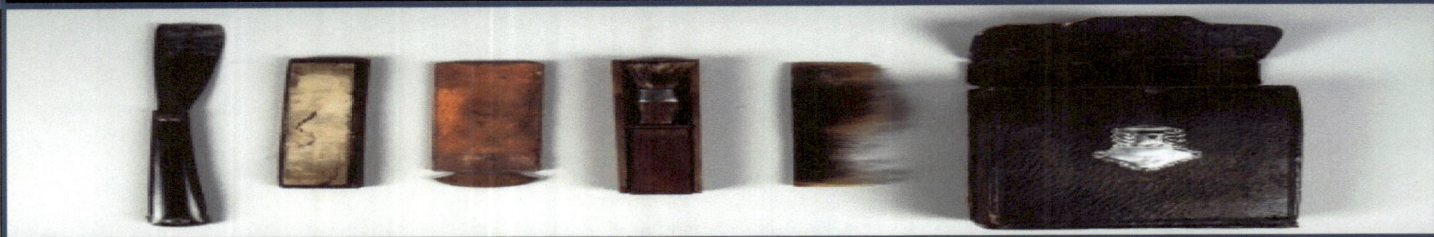

George Washington's Personal Shaving Kit with Brush Courtesy of www.mountvernon.org

"Looking good isn't self-importance; it's self-respect." ~ Charles Hix, Author

Face: Shaving
The Art of Shaving
Contact: www.theartofshaving.com

Hair: Thinning Hair
ROGAINE FOR MEN
Contact: www.rogaine.com

Body: Healing Soap
Keri Shea Butter Conditioning Therapy Lotion
Retailer: Walgreen's

Nails & Feet: D.Y.I. Mani-Pedi Travel Kit
Beauty School Mani-Pedi Kit—SBS-156990
Retailer: Sallybeauty.com

Scents: Classic Scents for Men
Paco Rabanne: www.pacorabanne.com
Karl Lagerfeld at Macy's: www.macys.com

Internet Grooming Tips:

The Grooming Lounge: www.groominglounge.com
Shaving Straight and Safe: https://shavestraightandsafe.com/2016/11/07/the-guide-to-18th-century-shaving

DESTINATION LAS VEGAS: Arts & Culture Calendar

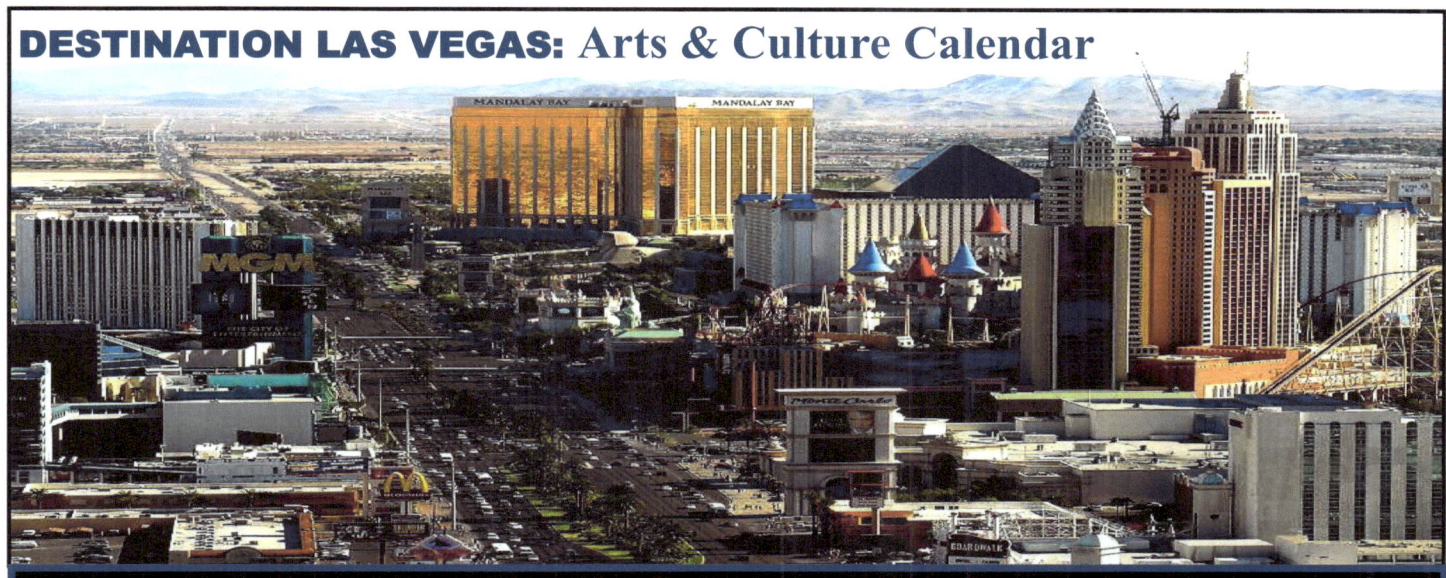

Arts & Culture Biographies Comedy Dancing Film Live Performances Music News Theatre Screen Stage

~ VEGAS ATTRACTIONS & PERFORMANCES ~

Las Vegas Mob Museum

300 Stewart Avenue
Las Vegas, NV 89101
Website: themobmuseum.org / Telephone: (702) 229-2734

THE SMITH'S CENTER for the PERFORMING ARTS

361 Symphony Park Avenue Las Vegas, NV 89106
Website: www.thesmithcenter.com / Telephone: (702) 749.2012

The Dennis Bono Show

Live Interviews and Performances by Entertainers & Celebrities
Thursday's: Main Showroom & Box Office
Doors open at 1 PM & Show starts at 2 PM
Michael Gaughan's Southpoint Casino & Hotel
9777 S. Las Vegas Blvd. Las Vegas, NV 89183
Website: www.southpointcasino.com / Telephone: (702) 797-8055

The Spring Preserves "Boom Town" 1905

333 S. Valley View Blvd.
Las Vegas, NV 89107
Preserve Hours: 9 a.m. to 5 p.m.
Nevada State Museum: Tuesday-Sunday, 9 a.m. to 5 p.m.
Website: www.springspreserve.org / Telephone: (702) 822-7700

Wynn Las Vegas Encore Theater

3131 Las Vegas Blvd. South Las Vegas, NV 89109
Website: www.wynnlasvegas.com / Telephone: (702) 770-9966

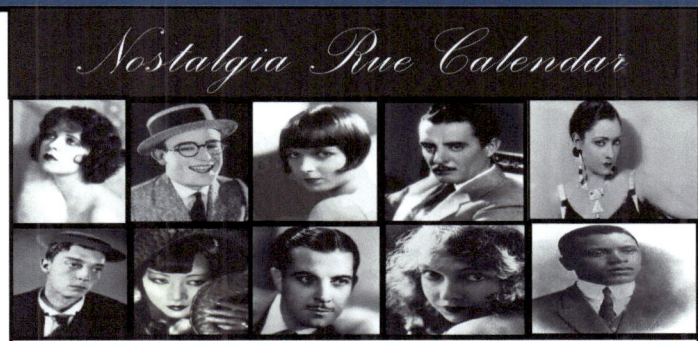

www.nostalgiarue.com
Copyright © 2018 by Mitzi E. Monroe

NOSTALGIA RUE'S ENTERTAINMENT MARKET REPORT

Books/Literature

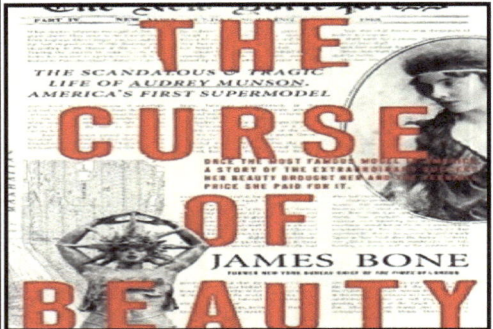

The Curse of Beauty: The Scandalous & Tragic Life of Audrey Munson, America's First Supermodel Hardcover – April 12, 2016 by James Bone (Author)

The tumultuous and heartbreaking life of a world-famous model whose riveting story of beauty, fame, passion, murder, and madness in the Gilded Age captivated a nation.

Movies/DVD

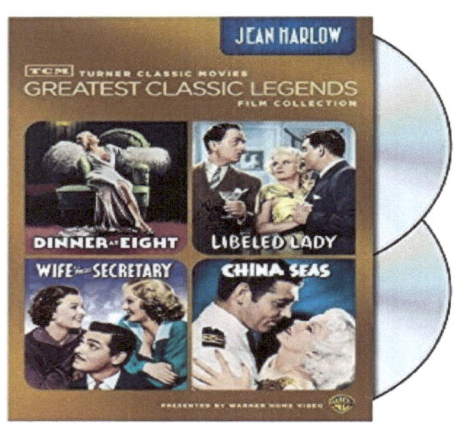

TCM Greatest Classic Legends Film Collection: Jean Harlow

TCM Greatest Classic Films Set includes 4 great films:

- Dinner At Eight (1933)
- Libeled Lady (1936)
- China Seas (1935)
- Wife Versus Secretary (1936)

Music

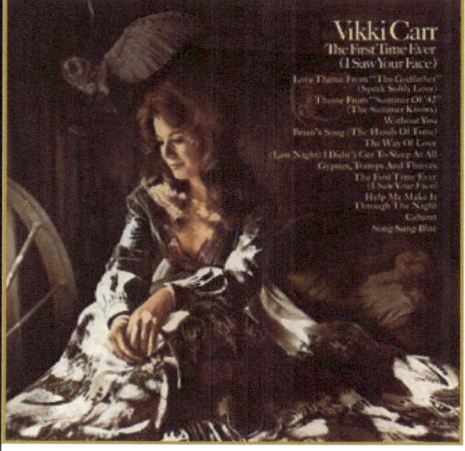

Vikki Carr: The First Time Ever (I Saw Your Face)

Sample selections below

Disc:

1 The First Time Ever I Saw Your Face
2. (Last Night) I Didn't Get To Sleep At All
3. Theme from Summer of '42
4. Gypsies, Tramps and Thieves
5. Without You
6. Song Sung Blue
7. Love Theme from The Godfather

All items are available at your favorite retail or online store.

Nostalgia Rue's Recipe Vault

Any Season Old Fashioned Comfort Dish

MITZI'S HOMEMADE SLUMGULLION WINTER STEW
(*Las Vegas, Nevada U.S.A.*)

1 1/2 # Beef Stew Meat, cubed and lightly dusted with flour

2 strips of Bacon (cut in small pieces)

2 Tsp of Olive Oil

1/2 Tsp of Butter

1 large onion, chopped

2 cloves of garlic, chopped

3-5 medium carrots, sliced

2 celery stalks, chopped

3 red potatoes, diced

1 bell pepper, chopped

1 can black eyed peas (optional)

1 can tomatoes, chopped

1 can Whole Kernel Corn

1 cup of Chopped Okra

3-65cups water

1 cup of chicken broth

1 tsp. thyme

Salt, Pepper, Creole Seasoning and Sugar to taste

Cooking Instructions:

- Sauté bacon in olive oil, butter with onions, peppers and mushrooms in stew pot or Dutch oven on medium heat until brown.
- Add stew meat to brown.
- Add and stir in the rest of the chopped vegetables before adding tomatoes.
- Add water and chicken broth stirring until mixed.
- Add thyme and seasonings to taste with a light sprinkle of sugar.
- Simmer with lid on for 1-2 hours or until vegetables are tender.

Top with chopped green onions or your favorite garnish and serve with corn bread or biscuits.

Note: Adjust your heat according to the pot and size of your vegetables and meat.

www.nostalgiarue.com. Copyright © 2018 by Mitzi E. Monroe

Nostalgia Rue's Favorite Classic Art & Culture

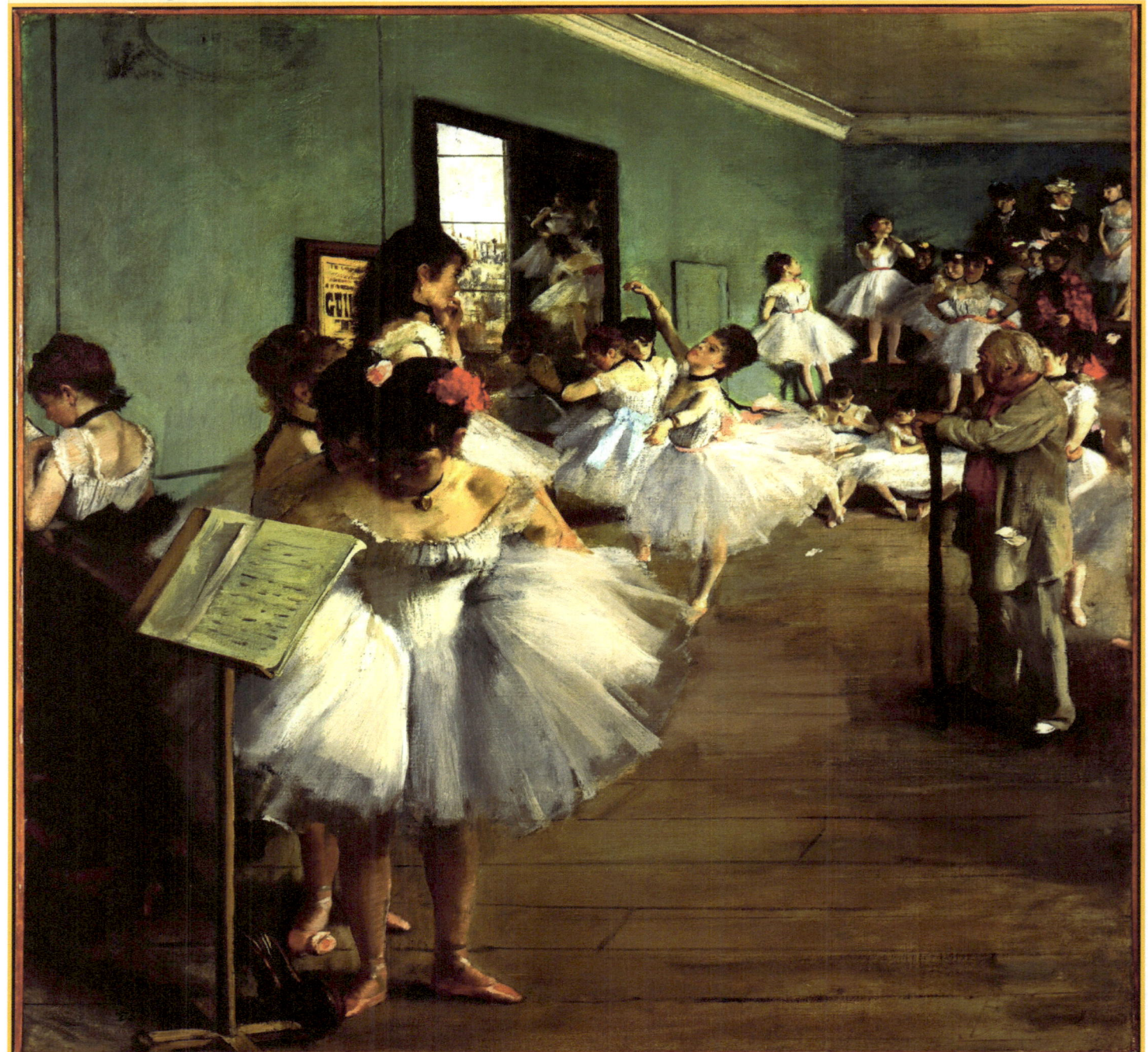

The Dance Class

Edgar Degas (French, Paris 1834–1917 Paris)

Date: 1874

Medium: Oil on canvas

Accession Number: 1987.47.1 On view at The Met Fifth Avenue in Gallery 815

On May 16, 2014, The Metropolitan Museum of Art announced they would make more than 400,000 public domain digital images available to the public for non-commercial use.

What's New? Creative Literature & Film

Literature

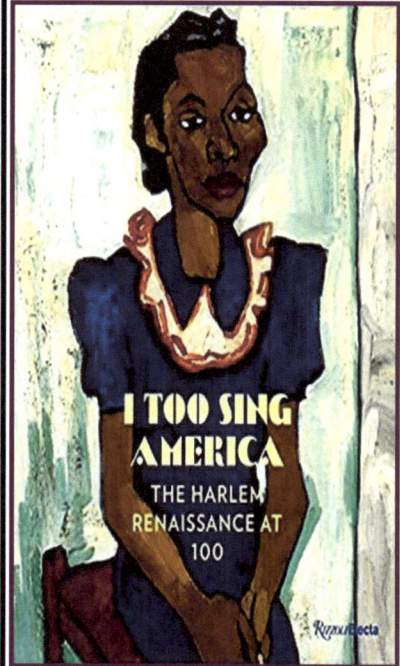

Nearly a century after the Harlem Renaissance (1920-1940) invoked a movement by multifarious Native Black DOS (*descendants of slaves*) and African-American artists, Wil Haygood, an acclaimed Harlem, New York historian and biographer reflects on nearly one-hundred years of the most acclaimed period in American history for black artistry and craftsmanship. This book is a library must have for lovers of well documented twenty-century life, American history and the architecture of a creative movement as experienced by the talented and courageous creative writers, painters, photographers, musician's, dancers and sculptors of that period that includes author, Henry Ossawa Tanner to sculptor, Selma Burke. A time capsule that preserves the integrity of artistry we must never forget.

Book Product details

- **Hardcover:** 248 pages
- **Publisher:** Rizzoli Electa (October 9, 2018)
- **Language:** English
- **ISBN-10:** 084863123
- **ISBN-13:** 978-0847863129
- **Product Dimensions:** 9.1 x 1.1 x 11 inches
- **Shipping Weight:** 3.5 pound

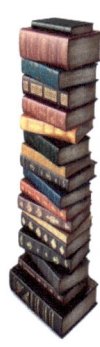

Movie

MARJORIE PRIME

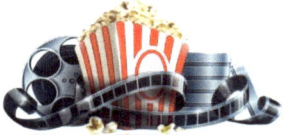

A service creating holographic projections of late family members allows a woman (Smith) to spend time with a younger version of her deceased husband (Hamm).

Starring: Lois Smith, Jon Hamm, Geena Davis, Tim Robbins and Stephanie Andujar.

Rated: NR

Genre: Drama/Suspense/Thriller/Sci-Fi Movie.

Running Time: 1:39.

Released: August 18, 2017

DVD: Yes

Movie Trailer: YouTube and Bing

www.nostalgiarue.com. Copyright © 2018 by Mitzi E. Monroe

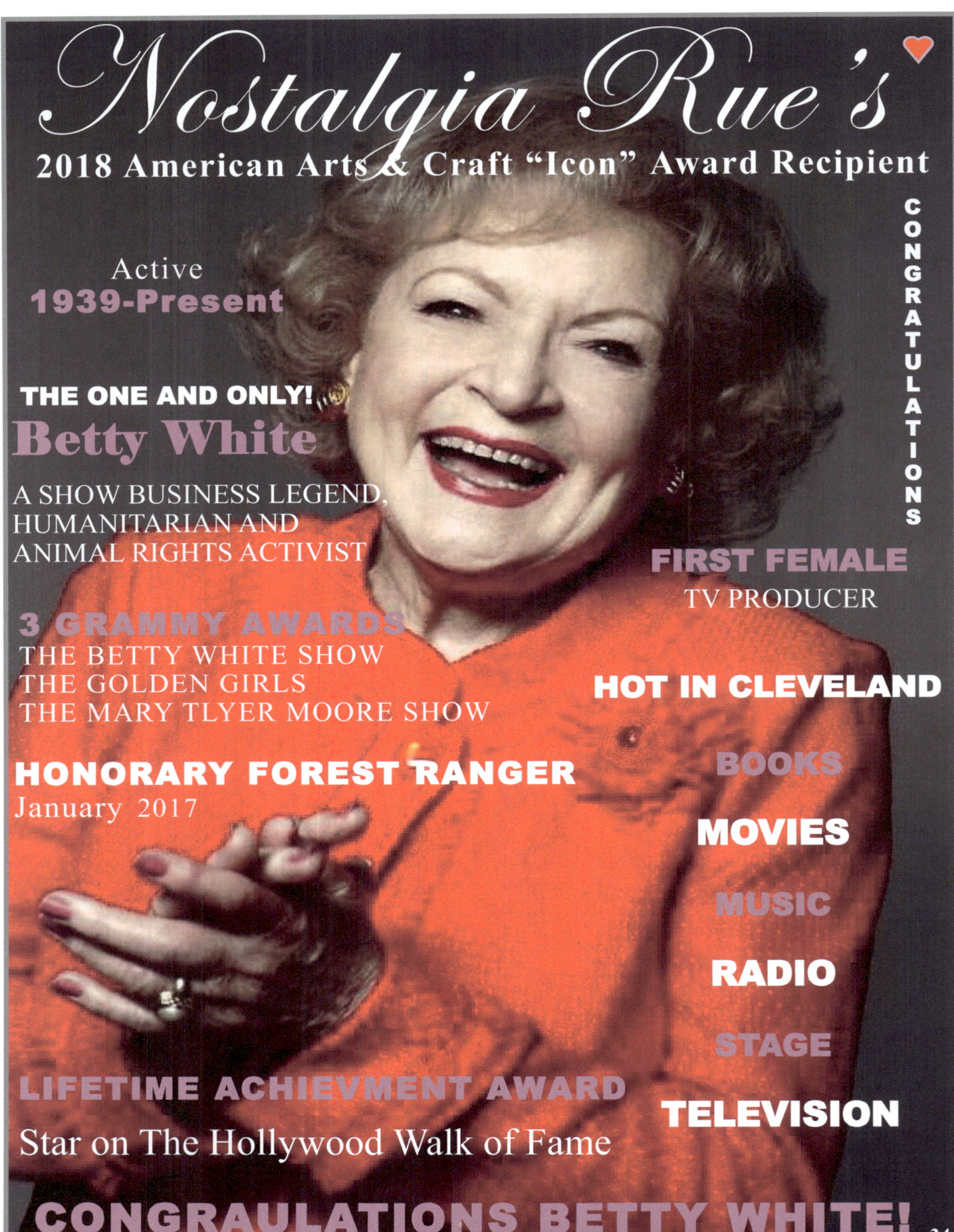

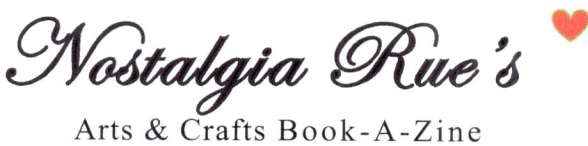

Arts & Crafts Book-A-Zine

Feature Story: Nostalgia Rue's First American Arts & Craft "Icon" Award

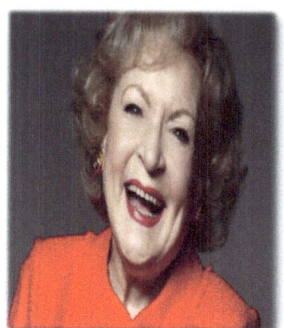

Dear Ms. Betty White,

Thank you for your humanity in the dignified delivery of showmanship that continues to make us laugh, reminisce and take brotherly love seriously for mankind, nature and animals.

Your contributions to your craft and causes are an exemplary measure of goodwill, kindness and generosity.

You are receiving this award for your fabulous legendary entrepreneurial contributions to entertainment, humanity and a lifetime of spirited animal activism, with a natural ability to:

- Bring joy and inspiration to generations.
- Contribute to humanitarian causes and the entertainment industry.
- Be an example to never give up and always give back.
- Hire good people and build solid relationships!
- Dispel ageism

Through your legacy of work, we are fortunate to have past, present and future opportunities to always be reminded that the human spirit is never too young to learn or too old to teach.

I can confidently say what many may never have an opportunity to say to you directly,

Thanks for all you continue to do. You are appreciated now and forever.

Bless You!

Mitzi E. Monroe, Founder

Nostalgia Rue

www.nostalgiarue.com
Copyright © 2018 by Mitzi E. Monroe

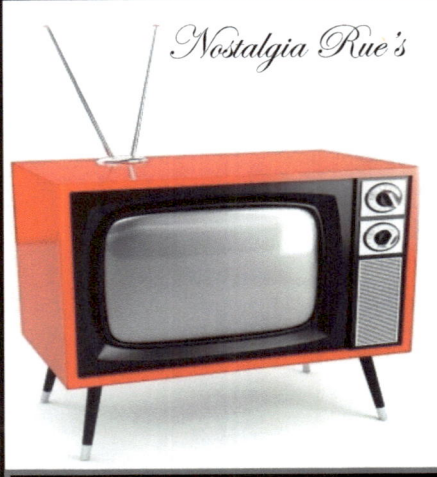

Nostalgia Rue's Classic Network Television Station Guide

**CHECK YOUR LOCAL CABLE LISTINGS
FOR CLASSIC TV CHANNELS & VIEWING TIMES**

1930s - 1940s - 1950s - 1960s - 1970s - 1980s

Comedies * Dramas * Movies * Soap Operas * Sitcoms
Talk Shows * Variety Shows * Westerns * Specials

Antenna TV
antennatv.tv

BounceTV
www.bouncetv.com

Buzzr TV
www.buzzrplay.com

Comet TV
www.comettv.com

Cozi TV (USA Network)
www.cozitv.com

Decades TV
www.decades.com

CLOO
www.usanetwork.com

Escape:
www.escapetv.com

Get TV
www.get.tv

Grit TV
www.grittv.com

Heroes & Icons
www.heroesandiconstv.com

ION Television
www.iontelevision.com

Justice Network
www.justicenetworktv.com

Laff.com
www.laff.com

Live Well Network:
www.livewellnetwork.com

Me TV
www.metv.com

Movies!:
www.moviestvnetwork.com

My Network TV
www.mynetworktv.com

Nostalgia Central
www.nostalgiacentral.com

POPTV.com
www.poptv.com

Retirement Living TV
www.rl.tv

Retro TV
www.myretrotv.com

The Cowboy Channel
www.thecowboychannel.com
www.familynet.com

This TV
www.thistv.com

TCM
www.tcm.com

TV Land
www.tvland.com

UP TV
www.uptv.com

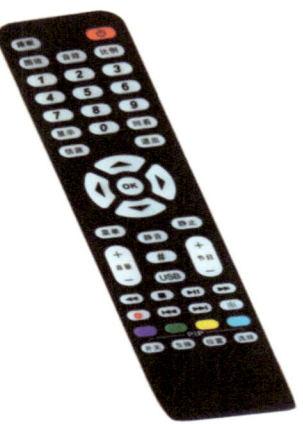

www.nostalgiarue.com
Copyright © 2018 by Mitzi E. Monroe. All Rights Reserved.

Nostalgia Rue's
CRAFTY ARTISAN™
~ Indie Arts & Craft ~
INSPIRATION DIRECTORY

Advocates * Arts & Craft Suppliers * Creative & Professional Development * Innovators

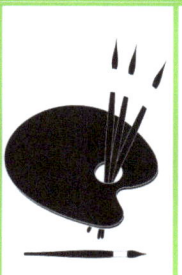 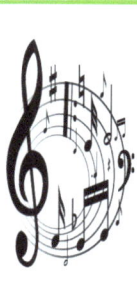 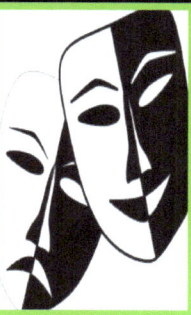 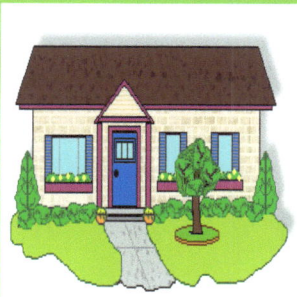 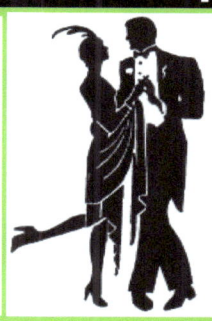  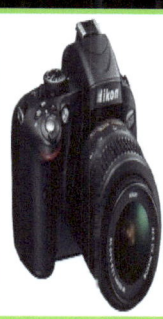

Information Local Hobbyist, Artisans and Crafters
Twenty-First Century Handmade DIY Creativity Renaissance Movement

Actor Artist Baker Books Creativity Culture Dance Fashion Film Fine Art Glass Graphic Design Interior Design Internet Media Metal Worker Mixed Media Movies Museums Music Network Painter Radio Sculptor Sewing Television Textiles Actor Artist Baker Books Creativity Culture Dance Fashion Film Fine Art Graphic Design Indie Interior Design Internet Media Mixed Media Movies Museums Music Network Painter Radio Sculptor Sewing Television Textiles Wood Worker Actor Artist Baker Books Creativity Culture Dance Fashion Fine Art Film Fine Graphic Design Art Indie Interior Design Internet Media Mixed Media Movies Museums Music Network Painter Radio Sculptor Sewing Television Textiles Wood Worker Actor Art Baker Books Creativity Culture Dance Fashion Film Fine Art Glass Graphic Design Indie Interior Design Internet Media Movies Museums Music Network Painter Radio Sculptor Sewing Television Textiles Wood Worker Actor Art Baker Books Creativity Culture Dance Fashion Film Fine Art Glass Graphic Design Indie Interior Design Internet Media Movies Museums Music Network Painter Radio Sculptor Sewing Television Textiles Wood Worker Actor Art Baker Books Creativity Culture Dance Fashion Film Fine Art Graphic Design Interior Design Internet Media Metal Worker Movies Museums Music Network Painter Radio Sculptor Sewing Television Textiles Actor Art Baker Books Creativity Culture Dance Fashion Film Fine Art Graphic Design Indie Interior Design Internet Media Movies Museums Music Network Painter Radio Sculptor Sewing Television Textiles Wood Worker Actor Art Baker Books Creativity Culture Dance Fashion Film Fine Graphic Design Art Indie Interior Design Internet Media Movies Museums Music Network Painter Radio Sculptor Sewing Television Textiles Wood Worker Actor Artist Baker Books Creativity Culture Dance Fashion Film Fine Art Glass Graphic Design Art Indie Interior Design Internet Media Movies Museums Music Network Painter Radio Sculptor Sewing Television Textiles Wood Worker Actor Artist Baker Books Creativity Culture Dance Fashion Film Fine Art Glass Indie Interior Design Internet Media Metal Worker Movies Museums Music Network Painter Radio Sculptor Sewing Television Textiles Wood Worker Actor Artist Baker Books Creativity Culture Dance Fashion Film Fine Art Glass Graphic Design Interior Design Internet Media Metal Worker Movies Museums Music Network Painter Radio Sculptor Sewing Television Textiles Actor Art Baker Books Creativity Culture Dance Fashion Film Fine Glass Graphic Design Art Indie Interior Design Internet Media Movies Museums Music Network Painter Radio Sculptor Sewing Television Textiles Wood Worker Actor Art Baker Books Creativity Culture Dance Fashion Film Fine Glass Graphic Design Fine Art Indie Interior Design Internet Media Metal Worker Movies Museums Music Network Painter Radio Sculptor Sewing Television Textiles Wood Worker Actor Art Baker Books Creativity Culture Dance Fashion Film Fine Glass Graphic Design Art Indie Interior Design Internet Media Metal Worker Movies Museums Music Network Painter Radio Sculptor Sewing Television Textiles Wood Worker Actor Art Baker Books Creativity Culture Dance Fashion Film Fine Art Glass Indie Interior Design Internet Media Movies Museums Music Network Painter Radio Sculptor Sewing Television Textiles Wood Worker Actor Art Baker Books Creativity Culture Dance Fashion Film Fine Art Glass Graphic Design Indie Interior Design Internet Media Movies Museums Music Network Painter Radio Sculptor Sewing Television Textiles Wood Worker Actor Art Baker Books Creativity Culture Dance Fashion Film Fine Art Glass Graphic Design Indie Interior Design Internet Media Metal Work Movies Museums Music Network Painter Radio Sculptor Sewing Television Textiles Wood Worker Actor Art Baker Books Creativity Culture Dance Fashion Film Fine Art Glass Graphic Design Indie Interior Design Internet Media Movies Museums Music Network Painter Radio Sculptor Sewing Television Textiles Wood Worker Actor Art Baker Books Creativity Culture Dance Fashion Film Fine Art Glass Graphic Design Indie Interior Design Internet Media Metal Worker Movies Museums Music Network Painter Radio Sculptor Sewing Television Textiles Wood Worker Actor Art Baker Books Creativity Culture Dance Fashion Film Fine Art Glass Graphic Design Indie Interior Design Internet Media Metal Worker Movies Museums Music Network Painter Radio Sculptor Sewing Television Textiles Wood Worker Actor Art Baker Books Creativity Culture Dance Fashion Film Fine Art Glass Indie Interior Design Internet Media Mixed Media Movies Museums Music Network Painter Radio Sculptor Sewing Television Textiles Wood Worker Actor Art Baker Books Creativity Culture Dance Fashion Film Fine Art Glass Graphic Design Indie Interior Design Internet Media Metal Worker Movies Museums Music Network Painter Radio Sculptor Sewing Television Textiles Wood Worker Actor Art Baker Books Creativity Culture Dance Fashion Film Fine Art Glass Indie Interior Design Internet Media Mixed Media Movies Museums Music Network Painter Radio Sculptor Sewing Television Textiles Wood Worker Actor Art Baker Books Creativity Culture Dance Fashion Film Fine Art Glass Graphic Design Indie Interior Design Internet Media Metal Worker Movies Museums Music Network Painter Radio Sculptor Sewing Television Textiles Wood Worker Actor Art Baker Books Creativity Culture Dance Fashion Film Fine Art Glass Indie Interior Design Internet Media Mixed Media Movies Museums Music Network Painter Radio Sculptor Sewing Television Textiles Wood Worker Actor Art Baker Books Creativity Culture Dance Fashion Film Fine Art Glass Graphic Design Indie Interior Design Internet Media Metal Worker Movies Museums Music Network Painter Radio Sculptor Sewing Television Textiles Wood Worker Actor Art Baker Books Creativity Culture Dance Fashion Film Fine Art Glass Indie Interior Design Internet Media Mixed Media Movies Museums Music Network Painter Radio Sculptor Sewing Television Textiles Wood Worker Actor Art Baker Books Creativity Culture Dance Fashion Film Fine Art Glass Graphic Design Indie Interior Design Internet Media Metal Worker Movies Museums Music Network Painter Radio Sculptor Sewing Television Textiles Wood Worker Actor Art Baker Books Creativity Culture Dance Fashion Film Fine Art Glass Indie Interior Design Internet Media Mixed Media Movies Museums Music Network Painter Radio Sculptor Sewing Television Textiles Wood Worker Actor Art Baker Books Creativity Culture Dance Fashion Film Fine Art Glass Graphic Design Indie Interior Design Internet Media Metal Worker Movies Museums Music Network Painter Radio Sculptor Sewing Television Textiles Wood Worker Actor Art Baker Books Creativity Culture Dance Fashion Film Fine Art Glass Indie Interior Design Internet Media Mixed Media Movies Museums Music Network Painter Radio Sculptor Sewing Television Textiles Wood Worker Actor Art Baker Books Creativity Culture Dance Fashion Film Fine Art Glass Graphic Design Indie Interior Design Internet Media Metal Worker Movies Museums Music Network

Clay * Culinary * Fabric * Glass * Gilding * Jewelry * Metal * Mixed Media * Metal * Paint * Paper * Typography * Wood

Nostalgia Rue's
CRAFTY ARTISAN™
~ Indie Arts & Craft ~
INSPIRATION DIRECTORY

Guide to DIY Creativity, Personal Development and R.O.I.
A Philosophy of The Indie Arts & Crafts Marketplace

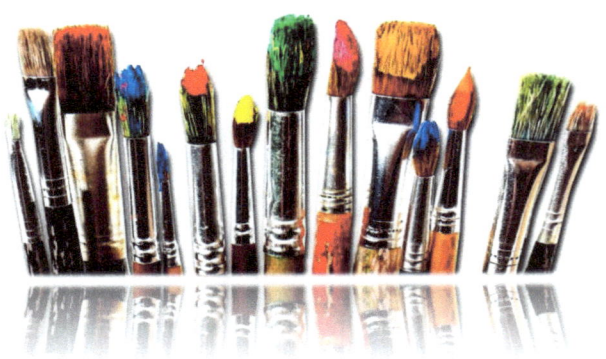

CONTENTS

The Crafty Artisan's™ Arts & Crafts Inspiration Directory 37

Books 39
Film 39
Internet 40
Media: TV/Radio/Podcast 40
Multicultural Art & Film Enthusiasts Multimedia Culture Series 41
Thank You! 42

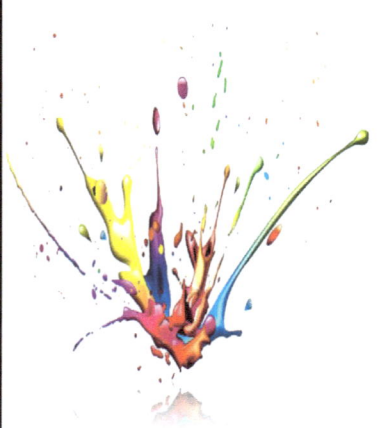

www.nostalgiarue.com
Copyright © 2018 by Mitzi E. Monroe.

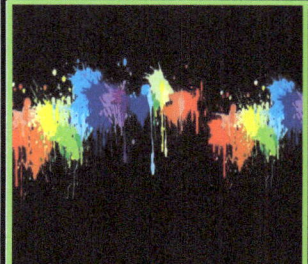 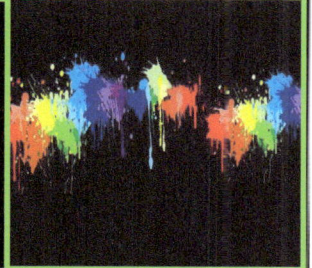

Nostalgia Rue's CRAFTY ARTISAN™
~ Indie Arts & Craft ~
INSPIRATION DIRECTORY

Fall/Winter 2018-2019 Recommendations For Arts & crafts Enthusi-

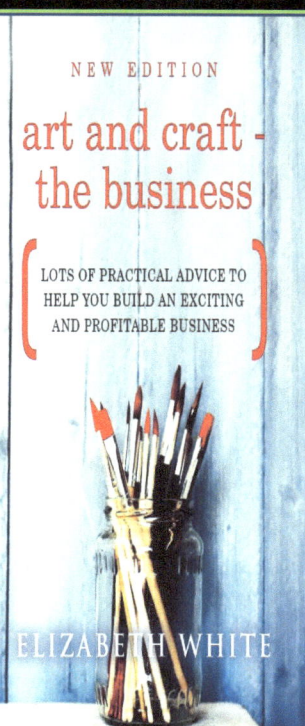

Book: art and craft—the business by Elizabeth White

This book takes you step by step through the process of starting and running a successful creative business. It has lots of practical advice on finding your market, pricing your work and using the internet to build a reputation.

Author Elizabeth White is an artist and gallery owner. She is an experienced business advisor, who has worked with all types of businesses. Some of these have gone on to become household names. As a writer and presenter of workshops for the creative sector. she is well known for her knowledge of the market and her method of communicating business skills to creative people.

Product Details:

Paperback: 192
Language: English
ISBN-10: 1871699061
ISBN-13: 978-1871699067
Product Dimensions: 6 x 0.4 x 9 inches

Film: Art and Craft

ART AND CRAFT starts out as a cat-and-mouse art caper, rooted in questions of authorship and authenticity—but what emerges is an intimate story of obsession and the universal need for community, appreciation, and purpose.

Mark Landis is one of the most prolific art forgers of the modern era and he isn't in it for the money. In the last 30 years he's copied hundreds of pieces, from 15th-century icons from Picasso to Dr. Seuss, he donates to museums across the country. When registrar, Matthew Leininger, discovers the deception, Landis must confront his legacy and a chorus of duped professionals intent on stopping him. But Landis, a diagnosed schizophrenic, driven since his teens to escape "the life of a mental patient," and ending the con isn't so simple. A cat-and-mouse caper told with humor and compassion, **Art and Craft** uncovers the universal in one man's search for connection and respect.

Release date: Apr 17, 2014
Directors: Sam Cullman, Jennifer Grausman, Mark Becker
Mark Landis: marklandisoriginal.com

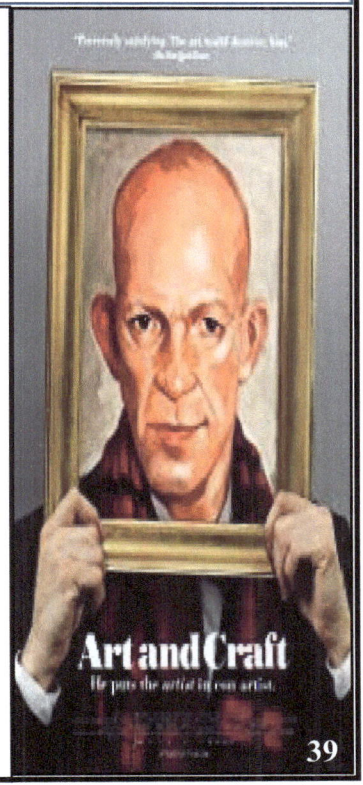

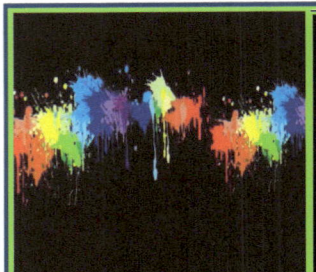
Nostalgia Rue's
CRAFTY ARTISAN™
~ Indie Arts & Craft ~
INSPIRATION DIRECTORY
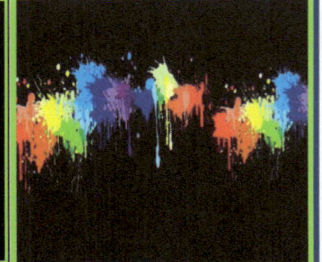

DIY Creativity & Professional Development Resources For Arts & Crafts Enthusiasts

INTERNET

BBC Arts & Culture: www.bbc.co.uk/arts
Bluprint: www.mybluprint.com
Craftsy: www.craftsy.com
Create and Craft: www.createandcraft.com
Creativebug: www.creativebug.com
Creativity For Kids: www.youtube.com/user/ArtsandCrafts/videos
Looking for an Arts & Craft Show: www.craftmasternews.com

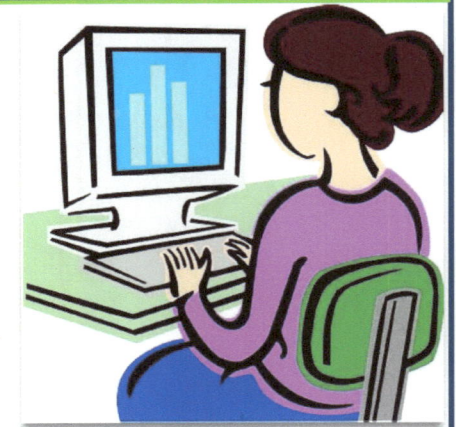

MEDIA: TV/Radio/Podcast

CRAFT IN AMERICA:

TV Listing: PBS (American Public Television)
Website: www.pbs.org/craft-in-america

A CRAFTSMAN'S LEGACY:

TV Listing: PBS (American Public Television)
Website: www.craftsmanslegacy.com

CREATE TV

TV Listing: PBS (American Public Television)
Website: https://createtv.com/ArtsCrafts

DEAR HANDMADE LIFE

Free iTunes Podcast (Archives)
Website: https://dearhandmadelife.com

DESTINATION CRAFT WITH JIM WEST

TV Listing: PBS (American Public Television)
Website: www.destinationcraft.com

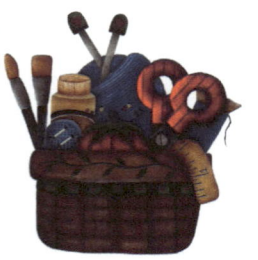

www.nostalgiarue.com
Copyright © 2018 by Mitzi E. Monroe

Nostalgia Rue's
Multicultural Art & Film Enthusiasts Multimedia Culture Series

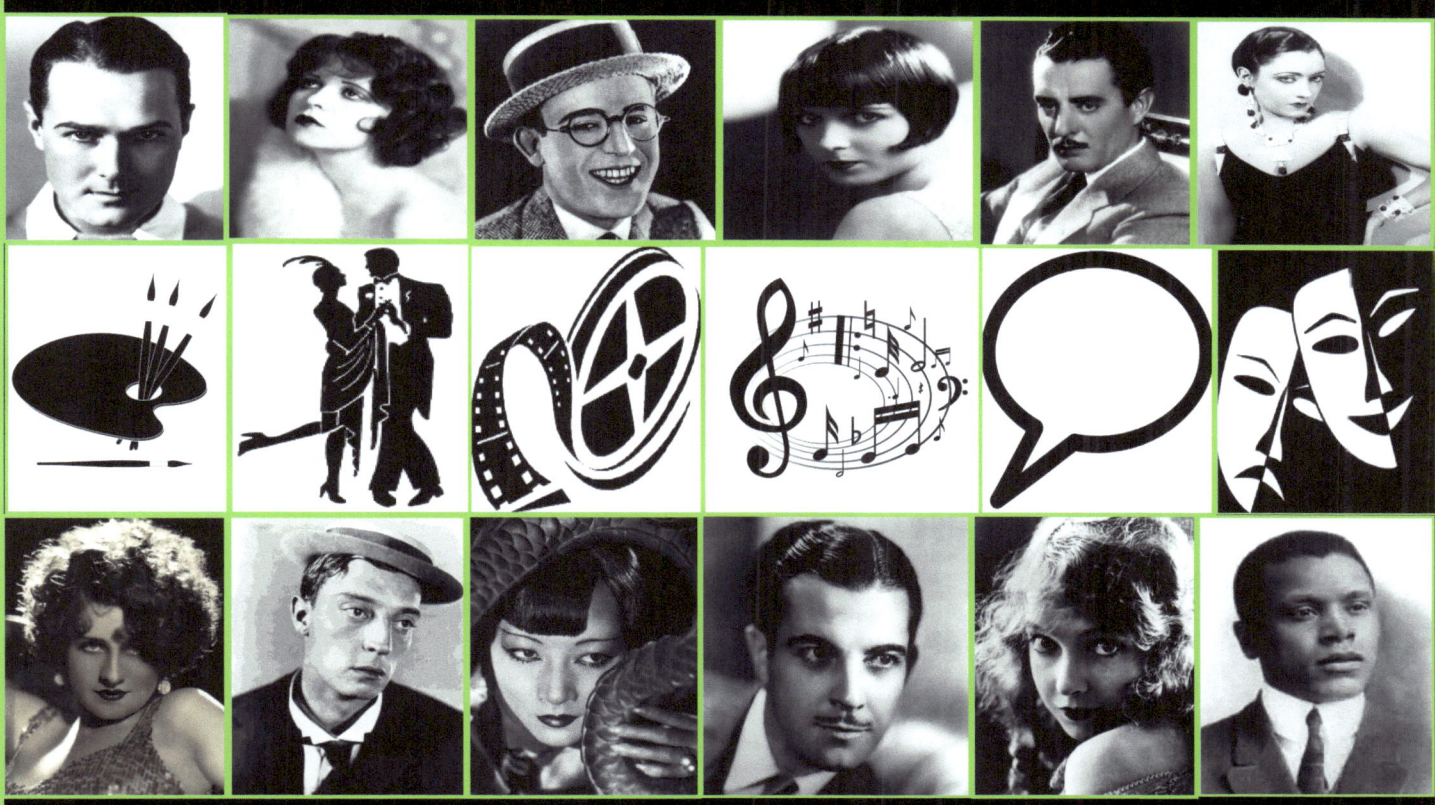

A Special Edition News & Notes

Narrated by

Mitzi E. Monroe, The Crafty Artisan™

Spring 2019

www.nostalgiarue.com
Copyright © 2018 by Mitzi E. Monroe

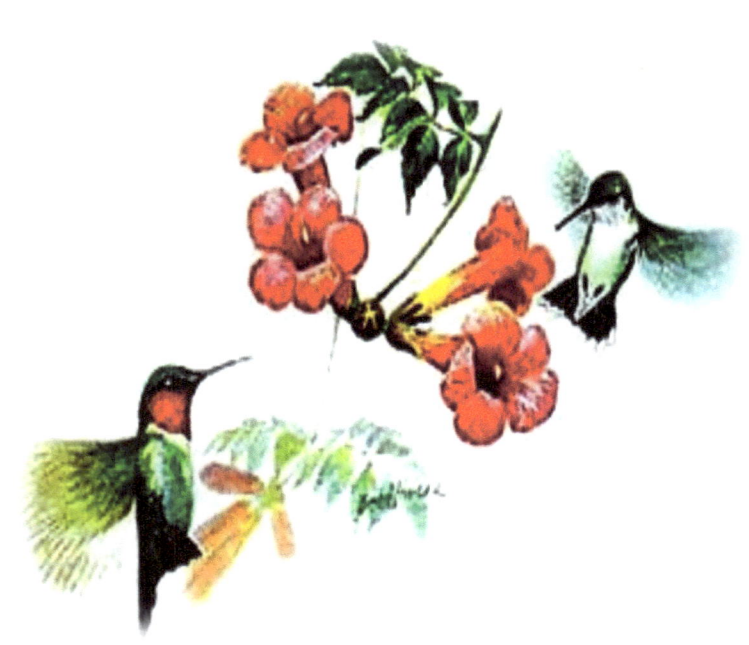

Thank You!

Mitzi E. Monroe

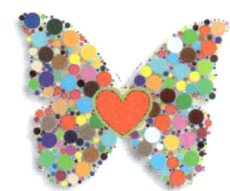

Nostalgia Rue
www.nostalgiarue.com

www.ingramcontent.com/pod-product-compliance
Lightning Source LLC
Chambersburg PA
CBHW040415220526
45473CB00004B/1253